The Shell Seek___

A play

Adapted by Terence Brady
and Charlotte Bingham

from the novel by
Rosamunde Pilcher

Samuel French — London
New York - Toronto - Hollywood

ISBN 0 573 11416 1

Please see page iv for further copyright information

THE SHELL SEEKERS

First presented by Kenneth H Wax and Nick Brooke at the
Royal Theatre, Northampton, on 1st September 2003,
with the following cast:

Penelope	Stephanie Cole
Olivia	Karen Drury
Nancy	Veronica Roberts
Noel	Ian Shaw
Lawrence	Timothy Carlton
Roy Brookner	Paul Chapman
Ellen	Jacqueline Clarke
George	Martin Wimbush
Antonia/Penny	Katherine Heath
Danus/Richard	Nicholas Osmond

Directed by David Taylor
Designed by Simon Higlett
Lighting design by Jack Thompson
Sound design by Clement Rawling

CHARACTERS

Penelope Keeling
Nancy, her first-born daughter
Olivia, her second-born daughter
Noel, her son, third-born
George, husband of Nancy
Lawrence, Penelope's father
Penny, young Penelope, doubling with **Antonia**
Richard, doubling with **Danus**
Roy Brookner
Ellen, Penelope's housekeeper

Time: around 1985 and in flashback from World War II
to the present day
Places: Gloucestershire, Cornwall and London

ACT I

Music. Like a front cloth, DC *hangs a huge framed painting of* The Shell Seekers, *a picture of young girls on a beach, looking for sea shells. At the moment the rest of the stage is bare*

The Lights change to show the painting as a gauze so that behind it C *can be seen a small white conservatory which is more like a gazebo in size and nature. This conservatory acts as a portal between scenes. There is an L shaped flight of stairs, the top half of which disappears into the wings*

The painting rises into the flies

Penelope enters, home from hospital. She carries a small overnight case. When she enters, she stops and looks with love around her home and then out into the garden beyond. Being February, the only birdsong comes from the crows and the rooks in distant trees

She remains looking out at her garden while the sounds of the birds abate as Lights come up on Olivia and Nancy who appear DL *and* DR, *on the phone to each other*

Olivia Someone should have been there.
Nancy She does have *Ellen*, Olivia.

These are Penelope's two daughters. Olivia, although not the beauty her sister once was, is in much the better shape, smartly dressed as befits her job as editor of a successful women's magazine, while her elder sister, once such a pretty girl, has long since lost her lithe figure and surrendered early to middle age. In contrast to her power-dressed sibling, Nancy is straight in from the Old Rectory garden, in much-mended quilted jacket, wool skirt and galoshes over her slip on shoes. She even wears an old velvet Alice band in her hair

Ellen, Penelope's housekeeper, now enters, carrying a larger suitcase and the inevitable plastic carrier bag full of personal items

Penelope turns and smiles at Ellen

Olivia (*insistently*) One of us should have been there.

Nancy (*lifting a leg to peel off a galosh; wearily*) Me—I suppose.

Olivia I am in *run-up*, Nancy. The magazine hits the streets in *three days*——

Nancy (*tired*) And I have to take Melanie to her Pony Club rally and somehow I also have to pick Rupert up from school and take him to his football match——

Ellen exits, hurrying off to do another task, as Penelope stands looking round at her beloved home

The Lights fade down on her

Olivia Mumma discharged herself from the hospital. You do know that?

Nancy Probably told the doctor a thing or two as well.

George (*off*) Nancy?

Nancy (*glancing off*) I have to go—there's George...

Olivia When did you say you were going to see Mumma?

Nancy I didn't... (*She stops herself in time*) I'll try and drive over tomorrow.

Olivia Yes, do. Because one of us really should have been there when she got home.

Lights down on the two daughters. The Lights come back up full on the conservatory, on another day. Penelope sits in her favourite straw chair reading a plant catalogue. She looks up and stares into her garden as if trying to remember it all

Ellen enters bearing a tea tray

Ellen Miss Nancy still outside?

Penelope For the life of me I don't know what she's doing. I have my suspicions.

Ellen If she could bother to come over today to see you——

Penelope It's all right, Ellen dear.

Ellen Not all right at all. One of them could have collected you. Been here to welcome you home at the very least.

Penelope (*having been through this before*) I really didn't mind.

Ellen Least you could have done was ring me. I'd have collected you.

Penelope I don't need collecting.

Ellen Coming home by yourself. In your state.

Penelope They wouldn't have allowed me home, Ellen, unless I was all right.

Ellen Hospitals? Nowadays? Can't wait to get rid of you, hospitals nowadays.

Penelope (*changing the subject*) What about those snowdrops? Have you *seen* the snowdrops? Spring is really on its way.

Ellen I'm sure. And tomorrow you'll be out there turning over the flowerbeds.

Penelope I absolutely love it when the first snowdrops come through. First real sign of spring. (*She gets up from her chair and stands at the open door of the little conservatory to look out on her garden*)

Nancy comes out of the house, armed with a pair of secateurs

Nancy You have far too many snowdrops, Mother. And you should have got someone in to cut your wisteria hard back in the autumn. I've pruned a lot of it back now—and don't look like that—it won't do it any harm.

Penelope But I don't want to cut it back.

Nancy (*putting down the secateurs*) It *needs* to be cut back, Mother. Otherwise it will go *everywhere*. You know what it was like last year.

Penelope I'm only really interested in this year.

Nancy looks at her mother sharply, hoping she hasn't heard right

Ellen, who has finished doing what she had to do, eyes Nancy with disfavour and exits

Nancy looks at her mother, unable to pursue this line. So she looks helplessly above her at the skeleton of the wisteria

Nancy I could pop over some time next week—bring George's heavy cutters. In fact before I go why don't I have another quick go with these... (*She picks up her secateurs again*)

Penelope leans over and takes them from her, putting them in her pocket

Penelope (*smiling*) You never can leave well alone, can you, Nancy? Now it's nearly half-past. You don't want to be late for George. And the children.

Nancy I'll pop over again next week.

Penelope That would be simply lovely. (*She kisses her goodbye*) See you then.

Nancy tightens her headscarf and exits through the conservatory

Penelope stands and watches her go through and out DL *into the darkness of the wings*

Dear Nancy. You always want to help so badly. And I'm afraid that's exactly what you always end up doing. And as for poor George—I don't know whether he just doesn't notice, or whether he ever noticed anything in the first place.

Nancy reappears further DS, *coming in to what is her own home, her old Barbour having been discarded, and with her hands full of two large gin and tonics which she carries in carefully*

She is watched by Penelope from her conservatory, on whom the Light gradually fades until she is just an observant shadow

In the DL *area a portly man sits reading his* Daily Telegraph *newspaper. This is George, Nancy's husband, a man much downtrodden by his motor-mouth wife*

Nancy has now reached where George is sitting. He makes a kind of Daily Telegraph *reader's hrrrumph! noise at something he reads as he holds out his hand for his glass, which Nancy gives him*

Nancy I was only trying to help, George.

George (*taking the drink from her*) Best left alone—where pruning's concerned, Nancy. Far best left alone.

Nancy I mean generally, George. Trying to help generally. (*She clicks her tongue*)

George (*almost apologetically*) I am *trying*—to read, Nancy. (*He samples his drink*)

Nancy This isn't a problem that's going to go away, you know.

George (*pulling a face*) And I do wish you'd buy proper tonic.

Nancy Ellen's not going to be the answer. Ellen only comes in three times a week.

George Ellen doesn't do the garden.

Nancy I am not talking about the *garden*, George. Don't you *ever* listen? I am talking about *coping*. How we are going to *cope*. I told you—I spoke to Mother's doctor, and he said she really mustn't and should not live alone any longer.

George (*eyeing her, worried*) I'm not sure what one's quite driving at here.

Nancy All I'm saying is that it would help a bit more if she took us a bit more into her confidence. Just for a start. That would make things easier. Give you some power of attorney for instance. That would really make things so much easier. I mean, let's face it—it's not as though Olivia or Noel ever as much as raised a finger to help.

George shakes his paper and glances at her, wishing to be left in peace

Can you imagine if she'd had her way and gone to live in Cornwall? I mean it's no picnic driving there and back there anyway——

George (*blankly*) To Cornwall?

Nancy (*crossly*) To the Cotswolds, George! Particularly in the sort of rain I ran into coming back. I hate driving in rain. I mean imagine if she'd gone to live in Cornwall. And I'd had to drive back in this. It simply doesn't bear thinking about.

George When you're shopping—get some proper tonic, right? Instead of this ghastly supermarket own brand muck.

Nancy Cornwall is over two hundred miles away from here. If—you know—if one was needed suddenly or something—Cornwall is a long way away.

George Know what the old man used to say about Cornwall. All frame and no picture.

Nancy We're going to have to do something.

George All frame and no picture. That's what he used to say.

Nancy I heard you the first time, George.

George (*looking up in some alarm*) You're not suggesting—are you? That your mother comes and lives with us.

Nancy Of *course* not, George. Trouble is of course she can hardly go and live with Noel. Or Olivia for that matter. But then at the end of the famous day—that really isn't our worry, is it?

George (*kindly*) I am trying to read my paper, Nancy.

Nancy (*sighing*) If only Daddy was still alive. Or Granny Keeling. Daddy's mother was the only person Mother would listen to. Granny Keeling always said I was the only person who did *anything* for the family. That everyone just took me for granted.

Nancy sighs again as George, having folded his Telegraph in two, puts it over the arm of his chair and searches his pocket for a cigarette. Something in the paper catches Nancy's eye and she picks it up to read the item

George How is that sister of yours anyway? Pretty as ever I'll bet. Pretty as ever.

Nancy gives him a look

I was just asking how she was.

Nancy George—someone is selling a Lawrence Stern—at auction—there's a whole piece about it here. Didn't you see this? Have you seen the estimate, George? (*She dandles the paper in front of George*)

He stares at it

Sotheby's do not get it wrong, George. Not Sotheby's.

George's eyes widen

You mean you didn't see this?

George takes the paper back and stares at it

Lights down on Nancy and George who exit. The conservatory is struck

Lights up on Penelope who stands us looking into the distance. There is the sound of the sea, and of gulls calling over and over again

Penelope Cornwall. Why people say it's all frame and no picture I have no idea. (*With a fond smile*) That certainly wasn't how Papa saw it. How we all loved Cornwall. And what wonderful times we had there. (*Her expression changes*) I remember it all as if it were yesterday—every single day it seems. Most of all I remember the day in September that was to change all our lives. I was on my way to the studio to bring Papa home for lunch——

From upstage of her, as if from inside her, Penny, her 19-year-old younger self, appears, as if wandering along a street, eating some chocolate, before stopping and looking up as if listening to something above her. She frowns and stands to listen

When I heard the news through the open studio window——

By now Lights are coming up on an area where a man, Lawrence, is standing by an easel and paint table. He is a tall, handsome man in his early seventies, browned by the sea sun, bright blue-eyed, dressed in faded old red canvas trousers, a white tennis shirt and a worn green corduroy jacket. His hair is snow-white and his hands already twisted with the arthritis that is going to cripple him. He has already turned his wireless on and is listening to the end of Chamberlain's announcement of war

A fisherman's net hangs from overhead and against a chair two surfboards rest, over which a striped bathing towel has been tossed. The cyclorama turns the colour of a sea sky

Penelope stands watching him as the volume of Chamberlain's famous broadcast increases to audibility

Voice (*on the radio*) "I have to tell you now that no such undertaking has been received and that consequently this country is at war with Germany".

Penelope shakes her head sadly and sits while Penny, still frowning at what she has heard, continues on her way—breaking into a run

Penny Papa? (*Stuffing her bar of chocolate into her pocket, she hurries into her father's studio*)

Lawrence has turned the wireless off

Penelope Papa...

Lawrence does not reply, then suddenly comes to

Penny Papa, I just heard the news. From your window——
Lawrence (*gruffly*) You've always got your mouth full. What are you eating now?
Penny Chocolate peppermint.
Lawrence You'll ruin your appetite.
Penny So there *is* going to be a war.
Lawrence Of course there is. I told you there was. (*He looks at her*) Well?
Penny Lunch. Mamma's made a ragoût. We're to go straight home——
Lawrence (*wryly*) And not go into the pub for a drink.
Penny And not go into the pub for a drink. (*She goes to the window to take Lawrence's arm*)
Lawrence No. I don't want to go yet.

Penny looks at him, then out of the window, trying to come to terms with the news of the war

Penny I really didn't believe you when you said there was going to be a war.
Lawrence You get some things right when you reach my age.
Penny Think it's going to be a long war?
Lawrence Long or short—what's the difference? Here we go again.

Penny looks at him, but he doesn't look at her. He's still with his memories. Penny starts to browse through some of his old canvases

Penny In the last war——
Lawrence What about it?
Penny You never painted anything, did you? War pictures I mean.

Lawrence looks at her as if about to explain then decides against it

Lawrence If we're not to go to the pub—we can have a quick drink here. There's a bottle of gin under that sand bucket. And a couple of clean glasses somewhere——

Penny All your friends painted. (*She fetches the gin out and collects the glasses off his paint table as well as a bottle of tonic water*)

Lawrence They're them. I'm me. I'm not that sort of painter.

Penny (*undoing the tonic*) You weren't any sort of soldier either. You still joined up.

Lawrence I was too old to fight. That's why I drove ambulances.

Penny But even if you'd been young enough—I still can't see you actually killing anyone. (*She places her father's glass in his hand*)

Lawrence It's a bit different this time. Didn't have Herr Hitler last time. (*He drinks*)

Penny (*looking at the painting*) Wasn't Mamma beautiful?

Lawrence She still is.

Penny But when she was *young*—how old was she when you first met her?

Lawrence Sixteen.

Penny Imagine. If she hadn't followed you to London.

Lawrence There'd be no you.

Penny Mamma always says you only married her because she could darn.

Lawrence Your mother was the first woman I really loved. That was why I married her. She didn't look anything like that painting. She was like a little waif when I met her. Skinny as a lamp post. Never put on any weight, not an ounce, but we soon put some colour in those cheeks. And a shine to her lovely chestnut hair. Gave her some money one day to buy some clothes. Just sold a couple of paintings—and back she came in this simple little frock which she made look like—made her look like a woman for the first time. Child one moment, beautiful young woman the next.

Penny A beautiful young woman young enough to be your daughter.

Lawrence It was a little red dress. Very simple. Plain red. Short sleeves which showed the blonde down on her arms. Best of all she had bought a new black beret which she wore just so. (*He puts a hand to his head*) Looked so sexy in it I even made her wear it in bed.

Penny (*turning a fresh canvas his way*) Comme ça?

Lawrence (*staring at it*) Your mother certainly knew how to wear a hat. (*He rises*) We'd better move.

Penny (*drinking her drink*) We had better go and eat her famous casserole.

Lawrence (*staring out of the huge window*) Now van to van the foremost squadrons meet—
The midmost battles basting up behind;

Penny Who view—far off… (*She forgets*) Who view far off…

Lawrence   The storm of falling sleet

Penny   And hear the thunder rattling in the wind.

*Without looking at her Lawrence puts his arm round her and they both stare
into the distance as a rumble of thunder is heard overhead. Fade as the
rumble turns to bombs falling and exploding. The sky is lit by the Blitz.
Penelope, spotlit, stands up from her chair and also stares upwards
remembering. The cacophony changes to birdsong and the quiet of the
countryside*

Penelope (*remembering*) And all of London ... all of London littered... All
of London littered with—with remembered kisses...

*Penelope continues standing in her conservatory, looking out front as
behind her Ellen is tending to the plants*

Penelope plays this scene away from Ellen

None of them ever understand why I rushed off and signed on for the
Wrens.

Ellen You tell them, and tell them again. Then you tell them again.

Penelope They still don't understand.

Ellen Half the time they don't listen. That's why. They don't listen 'less it's
about their selves.

Penelope I'd gone up to London one day—with my mother. Pappa was
worried about her being stuck down in Porthkerris with no young
company—so he persuaded her to go up to London for what he called a few
days junketing. While London was still comparatively safe.

Ellen Before the Blitz. The phoney war.

Penelope I met this couple at dinner one night. The Friedmanns—Jewish
refugees from Munich. They told us what it was like to be a Jew in Munich,
when the persecution had begun on earnest. Up until then it was as if the
war was happening somewhere else. As if it concerned other people, not
us. That night I met some of those other people. And the next morning I told
Sophie I was going shopping and went out and enlisted instead.

Ellen I was the same. I wanted to join up—but my dad wouldn't hear of it.
Said it was unnatural. Just wouldn't hear of it.

Penelope Nancy's the same. She maintains women who want to fight are like
a third sex. But that's because she's never been in that sort of position.

Ellen That's it. That's because they never been in that sort of position.

Penelope continues to stare into the middle distance as Ellen glances at her

*The Lights fade on them and up comes the sound of voices and the clatter
of a busy restaurant. Lights up on a table* DS *where Olivia, power dressed
as always and wearing glasses, sits checking some paperwork while she
waits*

Penelope, from her vantage point, now turns her attention to the new area

Nancy enters, hurrying because she is late. She takes off her headscarf, stuffs it in the pocket of her quilted coat, takes the coat off and slings it on the back of the chair

Penelope disappears into the darkness

Nancy Bloody train was late. Sorry.

Olivia (*putting her papers away*) It's OK. I just don't have very long.

Nancy (*sarcastically*) When do you?

Olivia I got you a gin and tonic.

Nancy A glass of white wine would have been fine.

Olivia (*looking round for the waiter*) I'll change it.

Nancy A gin and tonic's fine.

Olivia (*pouring herself some more Perrier and taking off her designer glasses*) So how was Mumma?

Nancy (*tidying her hair with her fingers*) Mother was fine.

Olivia So what's that look for?

Nancy I do wish you wouldn't *still* call her Mumma. It's so babyish.

Olivia I do wish you wouldn't call her Mother. It sounds so fogeyish.

Nancy She would rather have liked you to have gone and seen her in hospital.

Olivia I was putting the magazine to bed. She knows. I rang her and explained.

Nancy Now what are you staring at?

Olivia I do wish you'd let me send you to Michael.

Nancy My hair is perfectly all right, thank you.

Olivia If you like looking like a dead dahlia.

Nancy (*after she has drawn breath*) You do know Mother's doctor says she shouldn't be living alone.

Olivia If I were you—I'd get a second opinion. (*She sees Nancy's face*) He is just a country GP, Nancy. Much more sensible to talk to a consultant.

Nancy Olivia——

Olivia Anyway, Mumma said she doesn't want anyone living in. She's got dear lovely Ellen. And everyone in the village is devoted to her.

Nancy Olivia—everyone in the village is not a doctor. Suppose she has— suppose she gets ill again?

Olivia We'll get her one of those alarms you wear. We did a piece on them in the magazine—and they are *brilliant*. (*She eyes her*) But of course if you're that concerned—she could always come and live with you.

Nancy (*just about controlling herself*) I don't think Mother would like that.

Olivia (*smiling*) Mumma would hate that. The way you and George treat her you'd think she was senile—which she is not.

Nancy Seeing you haven't seen her in *months*——
Olivia I talk to her. All the time. I even called her while I was waiting for you. She's absolutely her old self. Told me her doctor's a complete idiot—and that if she had anyone living in it would end in murder. So *stop interfering*.
Nancy If it hadn't been for me, Olivia——
Olivia If it hadn't been for you, Mumma would have been living in Cornwall—which is where she wants to be.
Nancy Remember where Cornwall is, Olivia? It is light years away. Suppose she'd—suppose she'd been ill there? What would have happened then pray?
Olivia They would have done what they do everywhere else, Nancy. They would have admitted her to hospital. Treated her—and sent her home from there.
Nancy And we would have been miles away! That Cornwall business—that was all about her trying to recapture her youth, you know. I thought you'd have got that. You of all people. Her going to live in Cornwall would have been an unmitigated *disaster*.
Olivia What balls.
Nancy I *beg* your pardon?
Olivia I said what absolute balls. (*She puts on her glasses to read the menu*) Now. Let's see what we're going to eat... (*She offers her the menu*) Food.
Nancy I'd rather get this business about Mother out of the way first.

Olivia raises her eyebrows in pointed surprise but says nothing

For instance. For instance have you even given a thought to how Mother is going to manage her precious garden?
Olivia No—but Mumma has. With a firm of garden contractors apparently— who start next Monday. (*She looks at her stupefied sister*) She told me on the phone.
Nancy (*aghast*) Garden contractors cost a small fortune.
Olivia It's her money.
Nancy You haven't thought this through—as usual. Suppose Mother lives to be—well. I don't know. Ninety? Her capital won't last for ever.
Olivia (*taking her glasses off*) And that's what you and George are afraid of. Being left with a senile, destitute parent on your hands. Another drain on your finances after keeping up that absurdly over-large house you rattle round in and paying the fees for those ridiculously expensive and utterly useless public schools.
Nancy How George and I spend our money is our affair.
Olivia Ditto Mumma. (*She smiles*)
Nancy Do you know what's coming up for auction soon at Sotheby's?
Olivia One of Grandfather's paintings.

Nancy (*glancing at her in surprise*) You didn't know he was worth *that* sort of money.

Olivia Lawrence Stern is very collectable.

Nancy Yes—all right... (*Irritatedly*) But even if he is—what does that make Mother's pictures worth?

Olivia (*eyeing her*) Mumma only has one proper painting. *The Shell Seekers*. The two panels on the landing are unfinished works—but even so—I should imagine—let's see. I'd say they must be worth around about half a million...

Nancy (*stupefied*) Half a million? You *can't* be serious. Half a million pounds?

Olivia So you and George have no more need to worry on Mumma's behalf. Really you don't.

Nancy sits in stunned silence. Olivia checks her lipstick in her compact mirror

Have you decided? I really can recommend the goat's cheese salad.

Nancy I hate goat's cheese. Particularly warm.

Olivia I adore it. Every time I have it I think of last year in Ibiza.

The Lights fade to shadow over the restaurant table, leaving just Olivia's face lit as she remembers. Lights up on the UR *area. This time the light is clear, hot Mediterranean light. There is the sound of cicadas as well as the distant faint wash of a calm sea*

A lemon tree stands in fruit, beneath which are two deckchairs, one occupied by Penelope who is sitting reading

Olivia is still staring into the past, now focused on her mother. She stands and walks towards the sunbathing figure, still dressed as she was at the table, taking off her large fashion coat and hat and stripping down to a smart bathing suit. She ties a towel around her waist and stands to look down at her mother who is still absorbed in her book. Then taking a pair of fashionable sunglasses from her coat pocket, she puts them on and sits on the chair next to Penelope who now notices her

Penelope Nice swim?

Olivia Perfect. What's the book? (*She picks up the paperback*) You were well stuck in.

Penelope Oh, it's just holiday stuff. " The Perfect Holiday Read"—as recommended by your magazine's literary critic.

Olivia My ex-magazine. (*She runs some suntan oil on her arms*)

Penelope closes her book and stretches her arms out slowly

Penelope I thought you said you were only taking this time off as a sabbatical.

Olivia Right—but even so, while on sabbatical the magazine is my ex-magazine. You are an angel to have flown out at such short notice. I thought it might be well—easier. You being here—while Antonia is staying. You know how hopeless I am with The Young. Not that that's the only reason I asked you. Ever since I first set foot here I've been dying for you to come out.

Penelope I like Antonia. Never stops laughing and chatting. And so well-mannered. (*She pulls a mock gloomy face*) Wish Nancy's children were half as much fun.

Olivia (*laughing*) Mumma.

Penelope She really hasn't brought them up very well.

Olivia (*smiling*) Talking of children—how is my dreadful brother?

Penelope You know Noel. Haven't seen him in months. I rang him the other day to see if he was still alive and he said he was thinking of giving up his publishing job and going into advertising. (*She pulls a face*) He's also found himself a new flat in Fulham he can't possibly afford and was just off to Cowes for the weekend.

Olivia That's Noel.

Penelope He's very different to you. The absolute opposite.

Olivia smiles at her mother then gets up

Olivia More wine?

Penelope Yes, *please*. (*She gets up*) And by the way, I think your man—your Cosmo—I think he's lovely. I think you're a very lucky girl.

Olivia (*anxiously*) I'm so glad. I thought you'd throw a blue fit when you heard.

Penelope I don't throw blue fits. (*She takes her drink from Olivia*) I can see what attracted you to this place. I can see why you've been so happy here.

Olivia Still—bit of bombshell for you—my so-called sabbatical. Really just an excuse to behave like a moonstruck teenager—to come out here and shack up with Cosmo.

Penelope I don't see the harm. You haven't stopped working since you left university. I've been worried about you. Seeing how hard you work. You need to take it a bit easy.

Olivia (*smiling*) I like my work.

Penelope There are other things. It's all right—I'm not going to say it.

Olivia There's plenty of time, Mamma.

Penelope No, there isn't, Olivia.

Olivia looks at her, trying to hide her concern

(*After a pause*) It's only human. I'd love you to have children.
Olivia Cosmo doesn't have any *money*, Mumma. I'd never start a family unless I could afford one.
Penelope Cosmo has this lovely place. And you have some money.
Olivia Cosmo doesn't own this place.

Now Penelope looks at her daughter differently

He rents it. He doesn't own anything. He lives on a few investments he was left—and his Army pension.
Penelope I understand. But if you need some money at any time——
Olivia I don't, Mumma. We're fine. Honestly. But thank you anyway. (*She kisses Penelope*)
Penelope Are you in love with Cosmo?
Olivia You don't beat about the bush, do you?
Penelope I never have. I don't believe in it. Well? Are you in love with Cosmo or aren't you?
Olivia I don't think I've ever loved anyone the way I love Cosmo.
Penelope I know he's mad about you because he told me so. Now I know you've always resisted the notion of getting married… (*She pauses*) But? (*She drinks her wine*)

Olivia looks at her. Olivia refills their glasses

Olivia You're to blame, Mumma. You always said never accept an open invitation. Always have a date of arrival and a date of departure.
Penelope I don't think I was actually referring to marriage, Olivia.
Olivia I think it holds for marriage as well. And I made it perfectly clear to Cosmo from the word go—that this wouldn't necessarily be permanent— that I have to get back some time. And since Cosmo doesn't have the money to support us both——
Penelope You could write. Freelance. Or you could let me give you some money—to bide you over.
Olivia (*taking her hand*) Honestly, money's not the issue, Mumma. Promise. And as for writing freelance—I just couldn't. I'm not that sort of writer. I'm a journo who's become an executive because that's what I wanted. And I've been very lucky. I love what I do and I get paid for it. I need the conflict that comes with a demanding job—I thrive on the attendant pressures, and I love making decisions.
Penelope But does it make you happy?
Olivia Cosmo asked me exactly the same thing.
Penelope And what did you tell him?

Olivia Oh… (*She shrugs*) Oh, that the Bluebird of Happiness is an endangered species.
Penelope You don't really think that, surely.
Olivia When I'm working, I'm never totally unhappy. And when I'm not working, I'm never totally happy.
Penelope What a pity. You know—of all my children, I always thought you stood the best chance.

For a moment Olivia is not sure how to respond. Then she slowly smiles and wraps her arms around her mother, hugging her to her as if to assuage her mother's apparent disappointment. Over Olivia's shoulder Penelope looks thoughtful. The sound of someone approaching attracts Olivia's attention. She releases her mother and looks beyond the terrace to where the path must lead up from below

Olivia That's probably Antonia. (*She looks*) It is.

Antonia, a very pretty girl, appears, suntanned, in a short denim dress and round straw hat

Penelope Antonia.
Antonia Hi. (*A gust of wind seems about to catch her hat so she puts one hand up to save it, smiling at the two women*)
Penelope Good Lord. She looks like something straight out of one of Papa's paintings. (*With a happy laugh*) Gracious heavens.

Antonia stays that way—such a pretty sight—with her hand still holding her hat in place, isolated in a pool of light while the sunshine fades to black on Penelope and Olivia. Keep the image of Antonia while sounds of a party are heard, glasses clinking, raised voices, which fade under the loud burr of a phone ringing

The Lights cross-fade to DL, where a man in dinner jacket, Noel, is seen on the phone. He stands cigarette in one hand, phone in the other as he makes a call. He is a handsome man, but one who is identifiable at once as a rogue. He affects a very blasé, laid-back manner, even when ruffled

Noel (*into the phone*) That's right, Edwin. Lawrence Stern was my grandfather. I told you. You probably didn't hear me because you were too busy ripping off some poor old dear. Or not so poor probably. (*He listens*) I can't really talk now. I'm in the country, a rather good house party—for a change. But while I've got you… (*He pauses*) You saw how much they expect my grandfather's *Water Carriers* to fetch, dincha? (*He listens*) Right. At the very least. (*He listens*) As it happens we do—or rather my mother does. She has a rather large painting called *The Shell Seekers* and two other unnamed and unfinished paintings—they're on panels... (*He listens*) Of course they're Sterns. They're signed and naturally we have the provenance. (*Irritatedly*) But I don't think Mamma will be too keen to part with them. Not unless I can worry her with the old capital gains tax jazz or somesuch. But what about this—suppose any of my grandfather's oil sketches came on the market—sketches for some of his major works shall we say. Given the current state of the market what could one reasonably—what? (*He stops to listen and frowns*) Much as that, eh? I see. Right, Edwin—thanks. (*He listens*) No—look, I'm not saying they exist—I'm simply saying there's a possibility—and if it's anything more than that—yes. Yes, you'll be the first to know. (*He raises his eyes to heaven*) Deal. But first I have to find out if they exist—and then if they do—I have to get my hands on them. Somehow. (*He prepares to hang up*) I'll call you. Promise. Ciao. (*He puts the phone down and raises his eyebrows thoughtfully*) Well, well. Well, well—*well*. (*He whistles quietly to himself, takes off his jacket and bow tie and rolls up his sleeves*)

A loft ladder descends from the flies above him

Throwing his coat and tie into the wings, Noel looks above him then climbs the ladder. He disappears into the dark above just as a voice is heard calling

Ellen (*off; calling*) Mrs K? Mrs Keeling?

Lights up showing Ellen entering carrying a full log basket, calling anxiously for Penelope

(*Calling*) Mrs K? (*More urgently*) Mrs K! (*She frowns, puts down the log basket, dusts her hands on her housecoat and is just about to take off in search*)

Penelope appears with an armful of daffodils. Her mood is distracted, as if she has something on her mind—which indeed she has

Penelope (*edgily*) You don't have to go on red alert every time I disappear for a moment.
Ellen And you shouldn't be wandering around the garden not wrapped up.
Penelope I only popped out for a minute. To pick a few daffodils.

Ellen is standing staring

I need a vase... (*She looks around for a vase to put the daffodils in*)

Ellen It's all right… (*She takes the flowers*) I'll see to them soon as I've got a fire going properly. You really shouldn't be out in that wind. Changed direction since this morning. Nasty north-easter now. (*She begins to collect the materials for a fire*)

Penelope stands listening to the noises from directly above them. They both look up

I'd love to know what Master Noel is doing up there exactly.

Penelope I told you, Ellen. He volunteered to help tidy up the attic. He's worried about the thatch, apparently. Says there's too much junk up there.

Ellen Your insurers weren't worried. (*She checks her watch*) And as for that sister of his.

Penelope For once she has a good reason to be late.

Ellen (*sensing the mood*) Something the matter, Mrs K? There's something the matter, isn't there?

Penelope I'm afraid so, Ellen. You remember that friend of Olivia's I told you about——

Another mighty bump comes from upstairs as Noel dislodges something, distracting them both

Ellen (*looking up*) He'll be clean through the floor before you can say spoon. Which friend of Olivia's would this be?

Penelope The one I told you about—that nice man who lives on Ibiza.

Ellen I know. The one you had high hopes for. What about him?

There is a knock on a door, off. Ellen looks round in surprise

Penelope Good heavens—that can't be Olivia. Anyway, she said she was driving down——

Ellen I didn't hear no car. Did you? (*She looks out*) And I was right. There isn't one.

Penelope You'd better go and see, Ellen. (*She checks the time*) It can't possibly be Olivia.

Ellen Hardly. According to you, only time she's been early was when she was born.

Ellen exits

More rumblings from above in the attic. Penelope looks above her again and shakes her head wearily

Penelope And you won't find what you're looking for up there, Noel. I assure you.

Besides her emotional problem, something else suddenly troubles her, physically. Something which makes her take a deep breath, close her eyes and lower her head to her chest

She is standing like this and taking a deep breath when Ellen comes back in

Ellen It's a Mr Muirfield, Mrs K. From the gardening people.

Penelope Oh, good heavens above. Good heavens above—I'd forgotten all about him. Thank you, Ellen.

Ellen (*standing aside*) Come in, Mr Muirfield. Don't be backward in coming forward.

A young man, Danus, enters, not at all the usual sort of jobbing gardener. He is tall, dark-haired and good looking. He is also introverted and withdrawn, apparently truculent in fact

He stands for a moment behind Penelope who has turned back to stare out of the window

Danus Mrs Keeling?

Penelope Yes—I'm so sorry... (*She turns to greet him and the moment she sees him, as if everything else wasn't enough to cope with, it is as if she has seen a ghost. She puts a hand to her chest as if to steady herself*) Good heavens above.

Afraid she is going to pass out, Danus moves towards her

Danus What is it? Is something the matter?

Penelope No—no, it's all right—it's just—I'm so sorry—I just felt a bit... I suddenly got rather dizzy.

Danus Want me to call your... (*He looks helplessly over his shoulder*)

Penelope Heavens, no. Ellen would have the ambulance here before you knew it... (*She sees his look of concern*) And there really is *no need*. I'm perfectly all right now. It's just that I... (*She stops herself from telling him*) I forgot to have any breakfast.

Danus Right. (*Not understanding*) Not a good thing. Can I get you a drink of water or something?

Penelope I'm fine. Honestly. (*Slowly, with one more look at him*) It's just you're not at all what I was expecting.

Danus What... (*At a loss*) Right. You mean my age.

Penelope No, no—no, my age. (*She looks at him*) Things are so very different now. When I think of someone to help in the garden, I see—well ... someone older.

Danus OK. But I am fully qualified.

Penelope Of course you are. Otherwise you wouldn't be here. Anyway, I've read your—your thing—so I know what you've done and what you haven't. So really what I need to know—is whether you're going to be suited working here. (*She gets up and goes as if to the window*) Anyway—anyway, as you can see, the garden is not enormous. It's just under an acre, and all lawn and flowers. (*All of this is an effort*) I don't grow vegetables any more. And I don't have any fruit trees. Too much maintenance when you reach my age. But there's plenty to do. There always is in a garden. As long as you *like* gardening.

Danus I like gardening.

A car is heard pulling up outside. Penelope hears it

Penelope I'm sorry?

Danus I said that I liked gardening.

Penelope (*still half-distracted*) Good—good—so can we take it that you'd like to work here?

Danus (*shrugging*) Sure.

Penelope (*looking out*) There'd be no point in you working here if——

Danus (*cutting her short*) I really would like to work here, Mrs Keeling. Very much.

Penelope Good. Then how about...

She hears a door open and close

I'm so sorry——

Danus You were saying.

Penelope I think that must be my daughter... (*She looks off*) And I was about to say that perhaps you might like to start tomorrow.

Danus Yes. OK. That'd be fine.

Penelope (*after a pause*) Something else I meant to ask you. How did you get here? I didn't hear a car.

Danus (*shaking his head*) I cycled.

Penelope Don't the people you work for supply you with a van? I'd have thought——

Danus I don't drive. They offered me a van, but since I don't drive... (*He shrugs*)

Penelope What about all your stuff? Your equipment?

Danus I manage.

Olivia (*off*) Mumma?

Penelope (*calling*) In here, darling! (*To Danus*) I'm sorry.

Danus (*nervously*) It's OK. I really should go anyway.

Olivia enters, already in slightly tragic mode

Olivia Here you are. (*As if Penelope was ever anywhere different*) Oh. (*She sees Danus*) I'm sorry—I didn't realize——

Penelope (*greeting her*) Olivia darling. This is my daughter Olivia—Olivia, this is Danus—who's going to be helping out in the garden.

Olivia (*with a polite but tight smile*) I see. Hallo, Danus.

Penelope At least I hope he's going to be helping me out.

Danus (*like a trapped rabbit—looking from left to right*) Nine o'clock tomorrow then.

Penelope Nine o'clock will be perfect. (*She pauses*) Perhaps you'd like to take a wander round the garden, Danus—while Olivia and I——

Danus No.

Penelope Are you sure? There's no need for you to rush off.

Danus (*quickly*) No—it's fine. I have to be somewhere else anyway. For lunch. Bye.

Penelope See you tomorrow morning then.

But Danus has gone

Penelope looks after him while Olivia prepares to take centre stage. Penelope, mindful of the reason for Olivia's visit, turns her attention to her daughter

Olivia darling. (*She embraces her*)

Olivia What an odd young man. Is he going to be all right?

Penelope He's sweet. Just a little shy, that's all. Anyway—that's neither here nor there, darling. Much more important is how you are. (*She gives her another hug*) I am *so* sorry. I really am. What a dreadful thing to happen.

Olivia It's awful, isn't it. (*She pauses*) I didn't know how to tell you. I didn't *want* to tell you on the telephone.

Penelope It's all right, darling. It's all right. Don't give it another thought.

Olivia I thought I wasn't going to be able to get down today.

Penelope These things always come as terrible shocks. The most terrible shocks. Nobody thinks straight at times like these. (*She looks round*) And where's this friend who brought you down? I thought you said this American you'd met was driving you down.

Olivia He did. He has. When he saw how upset I was, he said he'd drive me down. Like it was his idea to wait in the pub—since he said I'd obviously want to see you alone.

Penelope (*taking her by one arm*) Poor Cosmo—he can't have been any age, darling.

Olivia No. No, he wasn't. He was—he was only fifty-nine.

Penelope And there hadn't been any sort of warning signs?
Olivia (*shaking her head*) Not as far as I know. He wasn't overweight—and
he was very active—for someone his age. He did smoke quite a lot—but
even so. Fifty-nine. Fifty-nine's no great age nowadays, is it?
Penelope No. No, I don't suppose fifty-nine's what you'd call a great age
at any time.
Olivia (*after an awkward pause*) I think we both need a drink.
Penelope (*still in her thoughts*) Yes. Yes, what a good idea. There's some
brandy in the decanter, darling. If you wouldn't mind doing it.
Olivia Of course. (*She goes to get drinks*) What was it someone said? He who
aspires to be a hero or something——
Penelope He who aspires to be a hero must drink brandy.

Olivia looks back round at her

(*Back to her original thought*) I liked Cosmo. And he just worshipped you.
Olivia Mumma. As I explained at Christmas—when we'd broken up...

*Penelope just smiles at her daughter the way mothers often do, as Olivia
hands her a drink*

I just hope it didn't give you too much of a shock. Telling you on the phone.
Penelope Of course not. When you're my age, people are always... (*She
stops herself in time*) This brandy's doing the trick. Really going to the right
spot. How about you?
Olivia Absolutely. (*She smiles*)
Penelope You poor darling. It really must have come as the most awful
shock. News like that always does. All you can do is wait—that's really all
you can do. You have to wait first for the wave to hit you. Then for it to wash
over you.

*Olivia has her back half turned to Penelope so her own reaction to the
situation is not visible to her mother*

Olivia Was that how it was with Pappa?
Penelope (*surprised*) With your father? (*Carefully*) No. No, I was thinking...
(*Beat*) I was thinking generally really, darling. How it always seems to be.
With people you love. (*With a small shake of her head*) I really thought you
and Cosmo might get married.
Olivia If we had—I'd be a widow now.
Penelope (*frowning*) Poor man. Poor you. (*She realizes*) And poor *Antonia*.
Olivia Yes. Yes, I want to talk to you about Antonia, Mumma.
Penelope Poor child. She must be bereft. She must be totally *bereft*.

*Another crash startles them from upstairs and halts the momentum. Olivia
looks up in horror*

Olivia What on *earth...*
Penelope It's all right. It's only your brother.
Olivia (*edgily*) Noel? What the hell is Noel doing here?
Penelope Sorting through my old junk.
Olivia (*suspiciously*) I'll bet.
Penelope He thinks the attic might suddenly combust—or whatever the
word is.
Olivia I really didn't need Noel to be here today. I really didn't.
Penelope (*reasonably*) It is his home as much as it's yours.

Olivia looks at her mother almost angrily then pulls back from the edge

Olivia I'd better go and fetch Hank from the pub—yes, I know.
Penelope Sorry?
Olivia A Yank called Hank. (*She smiles*) But he's not at all Hankish. He's
very articulate, intelligent—and extremely civilised.
Penelope And obviously rather sensitive. Off you go and fetch your Hank—
while I go and give Ellen a hand with lunch.
Olivia Just don't read anything into it—we're only friends, Mumma. We've
only just met.
Penelope Hurry up. I don't want lunch to spoil—it's roast lamb. Your
favourite.

Penelope exits

Olivia watches her, then finishes her drink. She picks up her coat

*Noel appears down the loft ladder from above. He sees her, curses her
presence without her seeing him, then continues*

Noel Sis? Oh, of course—Mum said you might be coming down.

They give each other a peremptory kiss

But where's the latest toy-man?
Olivia Don't be so rude. I left him in the pub... (*She does up her coat*) I had
to talk to Mumma in private.
Noel Don't tell me you're *pregnant*.
Olivia You're not funny.
Noel I'm not trying to be funny. You getting pregnant's about as likely
as——

Olivia About as likely as you being worried about the thatch.

Noel *Touché.* OK—OK, I'll level with you. You know one of Grandfather's paintings is about to go under the hammer?

Olivia I'm not really in the mood to discuss this, Noel...

Noel You will when you hear. It's *The Water Carriers.*

Olivia Noel—I have something to tell you... (*She is trying to tell him her news*)

Noel Any idea what it's expected to fetch? And if it fetches its estimate— or gets anywhere near it—can you imagine what this is worth? (*He now stands* DC *in front of the unseen fireplace looking above it at the unseen painting hanging above it*)

Olivia (*staring at him*) Mumma would die rather than let *The Shell Seekers* go.

Noel Maybe. But what about the famous panels? They're just hanging unloved and unnoticed at the top of the stairs here. It doesn't matter they're unfinished—they'll have a rarity value. And you do know the money you give away while you're alive is worth twice——

Olivia I don't want anything from Mumma. She's given us quite enough.

Noel I'm only thinking of her.

Olivia looks at him and checks her watch

Olivia I had better go and collect poor Hank.

Noel If she'd let me sell the panels on her behalf I could invest the capital for her.

Olivia No, Noel.

Noel turns to her, about to try again

(*Meaning it*) I mean it. Leave Mumma alone.

Noel (*shrugging*) If you say so.

Olivia is about to go, but Noel stops her with a hand on her arm

Even so—just out of interest—have you ever heard Ma mention anything about any sketches? Sketches Grandfather might have done for his big paintings? (*In answer to his sister's look*) I found this letter—never mind how. It was from some Edwardian parvenu who'd commissioned a Lawrence Stern. *The Terrazzo Garden*?

Olivia (*puzzled*) That's in The Metropolitan, New York.

Noel The letter specifically mentions preparatory oil sketches for the work. So if so for *The Terrazzo Garden*—what price the other big pix?

Olivia Where did you find this letter?

Noel Complete fluke. Remember Grandpa's moth-eaten old coat Ma was
livid about me lending Sara? Sara Hammond? I went through it first and
it was in one of the pockets.

Olivia Hence the sudden interest in the attic. And I don't suppose for a minute
you told Mumma.

Noel just holds up his hands in mock innocence

You're so bloody underhand. You always have been. Why don't you just
come clean and ask her?

Noel You reckon I should? Know what they're worth? If they exist, that is?

Olivia remains silent

Ten K each probably. No, easily in fact. So suppose—just suppose we find
half a dozen. A dozen. The old boy never threw anything away, remember?
I mean, you remember when Ma sold Oakley Street? Remember the junk?
If he made sketches then worry not, Sis—they will still be extant. They're
around somewhere. And say twelve at ten K a time—or let's get wild. Let's
say twenty-four at ten K a time...

Olivia (*icily*) It's all right—I get your drift, Noel. (*She stops and looks out
at the figure in the garden*) You're not to say another word to Mumma
about selling her pictures. I mean it, Noel. If you want to inherit anything
at all——

Noel stares at her, knowing she means it

I mean it.

Noel OK. So you mean it. (*He stares at her*) And you want to get out a bit
more, sis. You look like undercooked pasta.

Olivia I have every reason. (*She pauses*) I've been trying to tell you. You
remember Cosmo, don't you? Cosmo Hamilton?

Noel The ageing toy-man in sunny Spain? So? When I last heard you two
had split up.

Olivia He's dead, Noel. Cosmo died the day before yesterday.

Noel (*genuinely appalled*) You're kidding.

Olivia He had a very sudden- and massive - heart attack.

Noel glances automatically at the distant figure of his mother in the garden

Noel Jesus, I really am *sorry*, Olivia——

Olivia It happened right out of the blue. No warning. Absolutely no warning
at all.

Noel (*still musing*) What a bloody awful thing to happen. How old exactly was he?

Olivia He was only fifty-nine.

Noel looks out again at Penelope in the garden. They both do

Besides being quite awful—it's also quite complicated. For me I mean. Because of his daughter. Because of Antonia. She's a terribly sweet kid, but she is only just eighteen. She hasn't any money and so I said I'd try and help her. Try and help her get a job. Try and help her get started.

Noel Yes—well, that's what you do, isn't it, Olivia? Help the sick and the lame. I mean don't see what's it's got to do with me.

Olivia It just couldn't have happened at a worse time, that's what. It's very difficult. What with being into a new relationship——

Noel (*interrupting*) A new *relationship*?

Olivia Cosmo and I split up at *Christmas*, Noel—it had been going wrong for ages.

Noel So?

Olivia Nancy's been going on and on about getting someone to look after Mumma——

Noel Ah. And Antonia could help look after Ma—rather than you help look after Antonia.

Olivia (*staring at him, having been rumbled*) It makes sense. I really don't have the emotional space right now.

Noel laughs at her

(*Hotly*) I don't. And it wouldn't be fair on Antonia.

Noel (*seeing right through her*) Diddums.

Olivia (*toughening*) Look—just help me sell the idea to Mumma over lunch.

Noel And in return?

Olivia (*after a pause*) I'll see what I can find out about any sketches. Walk me to the pub and we can talk it over. Deal?

Noel You're the boss.

Olivia and Noel exchange a look of well-practised complicity, then Olivia takes his hand and leads him off through the little conservatory

Lights down there and up on the opposite DS corner on Nancy and George in their usual positions in their drawing room

Nancy (*outraged*) This girl is only eighteen, George. I mean *eighteen*?

George reads his paper, not paying much attention

She'll probably lie in bed all day and expect to be waited on, George. Rather than doing any *caring*. Particularly if she's just lost her father. But the point is Olivia really might have let me know. She might at least have talked it over with me.

Behind them as Lights come up in the conservatory, Antonia is seen arriving and being greeted by Penelope. Antonia puts down her suitcase and Penelope takes her in her arms for a gentle hug

George All that money. (*He shakes his head*) All for a few measly rotten daubs of paint.

In the conservatory, Penelope leads Antonia off into the house, with her hand in the girl's

Nancy It really wasn't fair, George. She could have at least discussed it with me. After all, I have taken on the responsibility of looking after Mother. So the least she could have done was discuss it with me—and then there's the matter of the *paintings*. Something else she didn't think it worth to discuss. Although she and Noel did. So it's a *fait accompli*, isn't it? According to Olivia and Noel it's done and dusted—*The Shell Seekers* and the panels as ruled by them—belong to Mother.

George You saw today's paper, I take it?

Nancy Of course I saw today's paper, George.

George Four hundred and eighty thousand quid. Nearly double the estimate.

Nancy I really think you should have a word, George. Because... (*She hesitates*) Because, I mean, if Mother does—well. You know. If Mother does...

George No if, I'm afraid, Nancy. No if about it all. We all will. Comes to us all. We all will.

Nancy (*with a deep sigh*) Oh, very well—*when* she does. Better? When Mother does—you know. There'll be all this perfectly awful inheritance tax—and as Noel said—we're the ones who are going to have to pay the tax——

George With your mother's money.

Nancy Will you just please *listen* just for once? Do you think Mother has any idea what the rest of the pictures and everything are worth?

George Judging from her insurances——

Nancy suddenly stops and stares at George

Nancy (*interrupting him*) I'd forgotten you arranged Mother's insurances.

George raises his eyebrows at her

For heaven's sake, George! If the beastly old *Water Carriers* has just gone
for nearly half a million, she's going to have to *reinsure*. If she can afford
it. And if she can't… (*She starts to smile*) I've just had an idea. I'm going
to ask myself to lunch with her. Think, George. Think.

George About anything in particular, Nancy?

Nancy Think *half a million pounds*, George. Think half a million *pounds*.

*Lights down on Nancy and George. The sound of spring birdsong and the
warm light of April as the Lights come up* C *and* US

*Danus sits on an upturned bucket, with a khaki rucksack, eating a
sandwich by the edge of the frame beyond which can be seen a cherry tree
in bloom*

Penelope enters with a basket full of cut tulips

Danus finishes eating and rises

Danus Hi.

Penelope whips round, startled

Sorry. I keep doing this, right? Surprising you.

Penelope (*smiling*) I'd forgotten you were coming today, that's all. My
fault—not yours. I'm just not used to seeing anyone working in my garden
on a Sunday, that's all. Actually, I'm not really used to seeing anyone in
my garden at all. Full stop.

Danus Would you rather I didn't come at weekends?

Penelope I'm more than happy with our arrangement.

Danus (*looking round*) There's quite a bit that needs doing.

Penelope My daughter Nancy was right for once. I do need help.

*They stand in silence for a moment, Danus too shy to finish his sandwich and
Penelope enjoying the spring sunshine*

Danus I love this time of year.

Penelope When you reach my age, you love every time of year.

Danus My mother's the same.

Penelope And your father?

Danus (*with a certain amount of edge*) My father is a very busy lawyer.

Penelope So as far your gardening skills go?

Danus (*shaking his head*) My mother doesn't garden. She hates gardening
as it happens.

Penelope But she doesn't mind you gardening. Being a gardener.

Danus shrugs noncommittally

It's only a guess—but obviously you didn't want to be a lawyer.

Danus half smiles

And my next guess is that your father wanted you to be—but you had other ideas.
Danus I really didn't fancy the law. Just not me. So I opted for Horticultural College instead. (*He pauses*) Your hawthorn hedge needs cutting. It's really overgrown.
Penelope Rather you than me. (*She bends down to pull out a weed*) I suppose in the long run you're aiming to have your own business?
Danus Makes sense.
Penelope Make some money too. Good gardeners are a dying breed. (*She looks round her garden*) Do you come from round here? I know you live in the area, but is this your original neck of the woods?

Danus gives her a look

I know—I ask too many questions. It's only because I'm interested.
Danus (*shaking his head*) My family's not from round here. They live in Scotland. We're not actually Scottish. That's just where they live. Just outside Edinburgh. My father works in Edinburgh. And I'm living in a cottage on Sprake Farm. Over near——
Penelope I know. I saw the address on your references. Isn't it really too far to bicycle? When it's raining, for instance——
Danus I enjoy biking.
Penelope Fine.
Danus Thanks.

He sees Antonia coming out of the conservatory

But I'd better go and make a start on the hedge. (*He hurriedly tidies his lunch things and makes to move*)
Penelope Aren't you going to stop and say hallo to Antonia?
Danus There's rather a lot of hedge to be cut.
Penelope Please. She's feeling a bit blue. She lost her father only a week ago.

Danus stares at Penelope, then at the very pretty girl walking towards them

(*Looking towards Antonia*) I know. I'm going to fetch us all a drink. You've got all afternoon to cut the hedge. And I've got some cold beer in the fridge—that my son left——

Danus It's OK—really.

Penelope looks at him as Danus looks at Antonia. She puts a pair of dark glasses on to hide the shadows under her eyes as she joins Penelope and Danus

Penelope I was just going to get us something to drink, Antonia. This is Danus, by the way.
Antonia (*flatly*) Hi.
Danus Hi.
Penelope Danus is helping me with my garden. What shall I get you both? Antonia?
Antonia A Coke. Anything.
Danus OK. I'll have a Coke as well.
Penelope You wouldn't rather a beer?
Danus I don't drink. I mean... (*Lamely*) I don't drink - beer.

Penelope looks at them both then goes back indoors through the frame

Danus glances at Antonia then pretends to busy himself with the contents of his khaki rucksack

Antonia (*without much interest*) You just helping Penelope out?
Danus No. No, this is what I do.

Antonia glances at him

I'm a gardener.
Antonia (*shrugging*) Right.
Danus (*after a beat*) I'm sorry about your father.
Antonia Thanks.
Danus Mrs Keeling told me. (*He starts looking for a mythical something in his knapsack*) It must be awful—losing your dad.
Antonia Yes.
Danus I mean—you know. When you're young.
Antonia I'd imagine it isn't too hot at any time really.
Danus (*nodding*) I know. But it must be particularly—particularly cruel when you're your age.

Antonia glances at him again

Can't imagine what you must be feeling.
Antonia I don't know what I'm feeling. Numb, I suppose. It only happened just over a week ago.

Danus (*after a pause*) He can't have been very old.
Antonia No.
Danus (*biting his lip*) It's terrible when someone in your family dies.
Antonia (*looking at him*) Have you lost a parent?
Danus (*shaking his head*) I lost my brother.
Antonia God. (*She pauses*) How awful.
Danus He got meningitis. He was a great bloke. Wasn't a thing he couldn't do—least that's how it seemed. He was older than me... (*He shrugs*) Fantastic at sport. Great bloke all round really. Then he got this virus and... (*He shrugs again*) You know. So I know a bit what it's like to lose someone in your family.
Antonia A bit? (*She frowns at him in wonder*) So what happened? That why you dropped out? You know—I mean ... that why you took up this. Gardening, I mean.
Danus Yeah. (*He thinks*) Maybe. Dad wanted me to be a lawyer like him—but I couldn't hack that. Anyway, I'm not like him—and when my brother died we sort of stopped hitting it off really. It's a bit better now. At least we speak.
Antonia My Dad and me always got on. We got on great. (*She drops her eyes*) We could talk about anything.
Danus Lucky you. I mean—I mean that must make it even worse. Sorry.
Antonia (*after a pause*) Penelope says the first time you lose someone is the worst.
Danus It is. She's right. She's absolutely right.

Antonia stands looking at him. The Lights go down

Danus and Antonia leave

The Lights come up. Overlay the sound of raised voices, as the family enter after Sunday lunch. Everyone is gathered, including Antonia, Penelope, Noel, George, Nancy and Olivia, all talking as they come in

Noel You saw what it went for!
Penelope I do wish you wouldn't all shout. At least not all at once.
Olivia It's Nancy and Noel who are doing all the shouting, Mumma.
Nancy Oh, for crying out loud, Olivia. Stop being such an infernal goody-goody. We are only trying to get Mother to see common sense.
Penelope Yes—well, you know what Mark Twain said about common sense. There isn't enough of it about to be common.
Olivia What you are trying to do, Nancy—you and your brother—is rip Mumma off.
Nancy No, we are not! We are trying to do the best thing for her!

Olivia The best thing for her would be to leave her alone. All of you.

Penelope I can fight my own battles, thank you, Olivia.

Olivia You are barely out of hospital, Mumma.

Noel Ma—*The Water Carriers* went for nearly five hundred thousand quid!

Penelope Do remember we have a visitor, Noel? Antonia dear—you must forgive the ill manners of my family.

Antonia It's OK, really. My parents were divorced if you remember. And not exactly amicably.

A pinger sounds on the timer on Penelope's wrist

Penelope My bag. I must have left my bag in the house——

Antonia I'll get it for you——

Penelope It's only my wretched pills... (*She sees Antonia about to go*) I think I left my bag in the kitchen, Antonia——

Antonia You did! I know where it is!

Antonia exits

Nancy More likely she's off to the bushes with that ridiculous Danus.

Noel Ma—if *The Water Carriers* fetched nearly five hundred K—what on earth do you think *The Shell Seekers* is worth?

Penelope I'd say an immeasurable amount. To me.

Nancy You have three Lawrence Sterns here, Mother. Not one. Not two. But three.

Penelope I can count just as well as you, Nancy. Thank you.

Nancy George says the least you must do, Mother—is get them professionally valued. Then if you still don't want to sell, have them reinsured.

George looks much surprised

Otherwise some joker's going to walk in one day when you're just out there gardening——

Olivia It makes sense, Mumma. The least you should do is get them professionally revalued.

Penelope Why? I don't ever intend to sell *The Shell Seekers*. It's all I have left—from that part of my life. From Cornwall—and Porthkerris.

Nancy Oh, thank you. Thank you very much. Seeing I was born and conceived there.

Penelope That isn't what I meant—and you know it.

Nancy So what did you mean, then, exactly?

Penelope I don't think you would understand.

Nancy Why not? I'm not stupid.

Penelope No—of course not. I don't expect you to see Cornwall in the same way that I do. Why should you? I know it means a lot to you.

Penelope breaks away from the group who disappear into the shadows US

Of course it does—but it means much more to me ... different people—different things ... and Porthkerris will always mean something special to me...

We hear the sound of seagulls cawing, and of the Atlantic Ocean breaking on a shore

Penelope stands to one side to watch her past unfold as Richard, a handsome young naval officer in the uniform of the Royal Marines, stands as if looking out to sea

Lawrence Stern in a cloak and a large black hat appears, as if having climbed up the steps from below. He stops when he sees Richard

Lawrence (*puzzled*) Good afternoon.
Richard Good afternoon, sir.
Lawrence (*frowning*) Aren't you the fellow we were introduced to this morning? With General whatever?
Richard Watson-Grant, sir. And that's right—I am. We met this morning. Down by the Fish Market.
Lawrence Now Admiralty property.

Penny appears by her father's side

Pen? Look who's here, Pen. Chap we met this morning.
Richard Hallo again, Miss Keeling.

Penny stops and looks. Just the way the officer is looking at her. Lawrence notices and smiles

Penny Hallo, Major.
Lawrence Here to look round the gallery, Major?
Richard If that's all right, sir.
Lawrence Course. Interested in painting, are you?

Lawrence goes through the conservatory, followed by Penny just ahead of Richard

Obviously you are. Wouldn't have made the trek otherwise.

*Penny draws up a straight back chair for her father to sit, which he does,
gratefully. Richard stands looking round him, taking in all the invisible
paintings*

Richard My mother got me interested in paintings. When I was a boy she'd
take me round the galleries with her——

Lawrence Least she didn't drag you.

Richard In the end I used to drag her. That's how I got to know Porthkerris—
long before I came here. I'd seen so many paintings of it. Its unique light.
The way it glares off the sea. Its peculiar clarity. I thought it was artistic
licence. Until I experienced it myself.

Lawrence Does have a magic. Never get used to it. No matter how long you
live here.

Richard Do you paint, Miss Keeling? Have you inherited your father's
talent?

Penny Not a drop. I can't even draw a box. I wish I could sometimes.
Sometimes when I see something beautiful—an old ruin against the sky.
The sun on the sea. Foxgloves in a hedge. Somebody's face... (*She steals
a look at him*) Something you think you won't see again. Not exactly as it
is at that very moment. That's when I wish I could paint.

Lawrence Only entertainment on walls, you know. That's all painting is.
Entertainment on walls.

Richard Some entertainment. (*He wanders round looking*) Stanhope
Forbes. Laura Knight.

Lawrence Painted that at Porthcurno.

Richard I always associate her with circuses. Russell Flint. A *Munnings*—
Thomas Millie Dow——

Lawrence Idea was to form a unique collection, you see. For the nucleus,
we all donated a favourite work.

Richard Marvellous. Wonderful. But no modern works.

Lawrence Works you're so busy looking at. They were modern once.

Richard Yes, of course.

Lawrence I like what's happening now. After this shooting match is over—
know what? Something tremendous will happen. In the art world. Just
wish I were young again so I could be part of it. Or just sit and watch. Watch
the young painters coming back here—which they will. They'll always
come to places like this—but they won't paint the bay. And the sea. Boats
and the moors. They'll paint the warmth of the sun. The feel of it. Colour
of the wind. The essence of the rain. Wonderful. Give my right hand to be
part of it.

Richard You are part of it, sir. Without today, there is no tomorrow.

*Richard and Lawrence look at each other. Penelope watches from her
vantage point on the sidelines. The Lights fade down on the two men*

Penelope I was never quite sure of the moment I fell in love with you. I think it was then. The way you looked at Papa—the way he looked back at you. Not that it matters. What matters is that I loved you so much it was unbearable. In fact sometimes I hated you for making me love you so much. Papa loved you too. He loved you like a son. He loved you because you astonished him—scaling Boscarben Cliffs at one moment then sitting down and destroying the Surrealists the next. Since losing Mamma, it was the first time I'd seen him really alive. You even got him playing backgammon...

Lights up. The two men now on chairs facing each other with a backgammon board between them, a game in progress

Lawrence How long you posted here? Course you can't say, can you?
Richard No.
Lawrence Can't tell me when we're going to invade Europe either, I suppose.
Richard Even if I could I wouldn't. Because you've only won again.
Lawrence Any more of that whisky you brought?
Richard Plenty. (*He produces the half bottle from his pocket and tops up their glasses*) The portrait in the sitting-room. Is that your wife?
Lawrence (*nodding*) She was a kid when that was painted. Just turned eighteen. An artist called Charles Rainier. Charlie and I used to go on holiday together. All took a house near Varengeville one spring. Meant to be a holiday but Charlie went mad if he wasn't painting. Took him less than a day. One of the best things he ever did. Course he'd known Sophie since she was a kid. Daughter of a fellow artist. Another great friend. Work much faster when you know your model. When you're close to them.

Silence

Sophie got herself killed in an air raid.
Richard Penny told me.
Lawrence Should have been me.
Penelope (*from the sidelines*) You always thought it should have been you.
Lawrence (*to Richard*) They were my paintings so I should have seen to them.

The two men carry on with their game as Penelope takes up the reminiscence

Penelope But Sophie said you weren't up to it. (*She pauses*) You were worried about your paintings—the ones you'd left behind in your studio in Oakley Street. One in particular. The one that used to hang over the fireplace in your bedroom. Things were beginning to hot up and there was a lot of talk about air raids. So you wanted to bring the paintings home. Bring them back to Cornwall. It was perfectly understandable.

Lawrence As if it mattered.

Richard Then with the greatest respect, sir——

Lawrence Don't bother. Heard it all from Sophie. And Penny. And for God's sake call me Lawrence, dammit. You see. See if only Soph had stayed in Oakley Street even so. That is if she hadn't gone out...

Silence

It happened in someone else's house. They'd all gone out to dinner with these friends in Hurlingham. People called Hitchins—great friends who lived in Oakley Street. They took Sophie. If she'd just stayed behind. (*He shakes his head*)

Penelope You'd have liked Sophie, Richard. And she'd have loved you. She radiated happiness as if she was wearing it. Papa used to say to her—when he saw the way she made people smile—"got your happy togs on today, Sophie", he'd say. How he loved her. And how she loved him.

Lawrence It was a land-mine of all things. Everyone had just finished dinner, they were playing cards when they dropped a damn land-mine on the house. They did that early on. The jerries. Dropped land-mines as bombs - anyway it blew the house clean out of the ground. Just a crater, that's all it left. A bloody great hole. Blew everything else—and everybody to atoms. So they told me. To kingdom come. Should have fetched the damn painting meself. Or just left it where it was.

Richard This was *The Shell Seekers* I take it.

Lawrence (*nodding*) It's hanging in the Gallery. I let them have it on loan.

Richard I go and look at it whenever I can. It's my favourite work of yours.

Lawrence Rather have Sophie.

Richard You can't make that sort of equation. Not really. Life follows no rules. Particularly during a war.

Lawrence Think a painting's more important than a person, do you?

Richard No. But at least we still have the painting.

Lawrence falls silent. He puts down his glass of whisky

The Shell Seekers was painted here, wasn't it? In Porthkerris.

Lawrence nods

On Marble Sands. The little girl on the left——

Lawrence Penelope.

Richard I know. The other two little girls?
Lawrence They're both her—all three little girls. Look carefully. They're all portraits of Penny.

Richard looks at him

(*After a pause*) You're falling in love with her, aren't you?
Richard (*after some thought*) No.
Lawrence See from the way you look at her——
Richard I'm not *falling* in love with your daughter.
Lawrence Ah. (*He sits back and looks at him*) Know about Penny, don't you? Know she's married. And got a child?
Richard Yes. Yes, I do. She told me—the first time we went out.
Lawrence Good.
Richard I had better go.
Lawrence Not on my account.

Richard, half out of his chair, stops and looks at Lawrence

Not on Penny's account either.
Richard But——
Lawrence Never won a battle—*but*. Penny know how you feel? Do you know how Penny feels?
Richard Yes. Yes, to both parts of the question.
Lawrence Then just don't get killed.
Richard I'll try not to. When the war's over. And if I survive—once her divorce is through and she's free to——
Lawrence (*shaking his head*) Couldn't matter. Not the point. Point is do you love each other.
Richard Yes. Yes, we do.
Lawrence Then set out the board and let's have another game.

Richard looks at him, then starts to set out the backgammon. Above them in the frame, Lights up on the little conservatory in which Penelope sits reading a letter written on thin yellow paper

Penelope "My darling Penelope, Your letters have all arrived safely and are a source of joy. I carry them round like a lovesick schoolboy and read and re-read them, time without number. If I cannot be with you, then I can listen to your voice. Now I have so much to say, and as usual don't know where to start. Perhaps the unsaid is what this letter is about. All that matters is that we should be together and eventually—sooner than later I hope—we shall be married." (*She stops reading and looks up, up above her as if to draw* *strength*) "For some reason I have no fears that I will not survive this war. Death, the last enemy, still seems a long way off. And I cannot bring myself to believe that fate—having brought us together—did not mean us to stay that way. In this life, nothing good is truly lost. It stays part of a person, becomes part of their character. So part of you goes everywhere with me—and part of me is yours, for ever. My love, my darling." (*She holds the letter to her*)

Below her the two men finish their game of backgammon. Lights down. In front of Lawrence and Richard the huge frame descends as the main Curtain. *Within it now is the painting of* The Shell Seekers

End of Act I

ACT II

The same. Later that afternoon

The big painting of The Shell Seekers *turns to gauze, as the Lights come up behind it. The frame is raised and disappears upwards*

Noel is seen standing DS *in front of where the fireplace would be. He is smoking a cigarette and staring at where the picture would be hanging as the frame ascends into the flies*

After a moment Penelope comes down the stairs, pulling her cardigan around her and giving a stifled yawn behind Noel's back, having just woken up from her afternoon sleep. She enters, taking a look around as she does so

Noel (*turning and seeing his mother*) Hi, Ma. Have a good ziz?

Penelope Yes. Yes, thank you. Where is everyone?

Noel Out and about. Nancy's outside grilling your pretty new gardening boy…

Penelope That just won't do. I really don't want Nancy interfering in my affairs…

Noel George is taking a post prandial hike—as he so lightly calls it, and Olivia is shut away in the study talking to Hank the Shank sur le jolly old telephone. And Antonia is upstairs asleep. In my bed.

Penelope (*eyeing him; after a good pause*) You had better stay well away from Antonia. I mean it.

Noel Antonia's not my type. Don't worry.

Penelope (*looking round with a sigh*) Somebody might at least have made a start at clearing up.

Noel (*back staring at the picture*) What was all that rabbit over lunch about Cornwall? The long and touching ramble down old memory lane.

Penelope I was actually talking to Antonia.

Noel And I couldn't help hearing. (*He turns back to look at the painting*) Want to know what I think? This isn't a bad painting. It's certainly far too good just to be hanging above a fireplace.

Penelope Well, that's where it's staying. Noel…

Noel Ma? (*He rids himself of his cigarette*)

Penelope Would you like to come to Cornwall with me? I want to go down
   to Porthkerris for a few days.
Noel Cornwall? (*He looks at her, embarrassed*) Come on, Ma. I'm a bit long
   in the tooth for building sandcastles.
Penelope We could go and see Carn Cottage—and your grandfather's
   studio. We could go to the Gallery. I thought it might be of interest to you—
   now that you've taken such an interest in art. And Papa's paintings in
   particular.

*Noel eyes her, with no answer to the deliberately low blow. He lights a fresh
cigarette*

   You know I'd rather people didn't smoke in here.
Noel OK. I'll take it outside. (*He turns away*)
Penelope (*quickly*) I want to go before the end of the month. Before the
   tourists.
Noel The end of the *month*? (*As if this was his reason*) What a shame. No can
   do, I'm afraid. We're up to our necks in the office—and I'm not actually
   due any leave till July.
Penelope We could make it one weekend.
Noel (*mock gritting his teeth*) No way. Not before the end of the month.
   Really.
Penelope It was just a thought.
Noel Late summer maybe—autumn even. Sorr-ee. (*He holds up the
   cigarette*) I'll finish this in the garden.

As Noel goes he crosses Nancy who is just coming in

   Finished interrogating ze gardener?
Nancy For all you know—or care—Mother could be employing a convicted
   serial rapist. Or a murderer.
Noel I'm sure you made him talk. You have vays of making everyone talk.
   All except ze dredded *George*. But then that's probably a blessing because
   I doubt very much if George has anything very much to say.

Noel exits

Nancy (*chiding, eyeing Penelope*) You should have taken my advice,
   Mother, and stayed in bed. You look tired.
Penelope Probably because I've just cooked lunch for six, Nancy. What
   were you doing out there? Bending poor Danus' ear.
Nancy (*sighing*) What do you *know* about this young man, Mother?
   Absolutely nothing. Other than the fact he can do a bit of gardening. What

I'm sure you do *not* know—for instance—is that his father is a lawyer? Not just a lawyer but he's actually a Writer to the Signet? In Scotland? And that his mother is the daughter of a peer.

Penelope Now you really have put the wind up me. We'd better call the police this minute.

Nancy Doesn't it occur to you that he might be a little over-qualified to be working for some hole in the wall rustic gardening service? I mean background-wise?

Penelope (*echoing the word to show its stupidity*) Background-wise.

Nancy A young man from his sort of background working for the agricultural minimum? I mean—really. *Why* is he doing it?

Penelope Oh, Nancy. Nancy you were such a sweet little girl.

Nancy Just stop to think for one moment, Mother. Danus doesn't drive—he doesn't drink.

Penelope Hardly any crime in that.

Nancy Perhaps not—but it is definitely *peculiar*. Perhaps because he has a *background*. It isn't beyond the realms of possibility that he might, say— he might have had an accident driving when he was drunk—even killed somebody—I don't suppose for a minute you checked his references. I wouldn't be at all surprised if you didn't. You're so *naïve*, your generation. Someone just has to *look* respectable. Here you have what amounts to practically a complete stranger, working in your garden with you all alone in your house——

Penelope There's nothing here of any real value——

Nancy Grandfather's pictures?

Penelope You can't just pinch and flog well-known paintings, Nancy. And besides the paintings——

Nancy All right! All right, forget about the wretched pictures and think about you! You never lock a door. You have no alarm. You're woefully under-insured——

Penelope You mean the paintings are. Why don't you just come out with it, Nancy? It's perfectly obvious you want me to sell them.

Nancy You could at least sell the panels, Mother. While the market's high.

Penelope looks at her with despair, then sits slowly in her armchair, closing her eyes

You don't just want to hand the money over to the government, surely?

Penelope You mean *you* don't. Anyway—I won't be here to do the handing.

Nancy I do wish you wouldn't talk like that.

Penelope laughs wearily

(*Wide-eyed*) I do. It's so—well. You know. Morbid.

Penelope (*eyeing her then shaking her head*) I was going to ask you to come away to Cornwall with me.

Nancy (*sighing*) You've got this bee in your bonnet about going back to Cornwall.

Penelope I know. I want to go back there just once. Before I die.

Nancy (*panicking*) You are not going to die. (*She catches her mother's look*) Anyway. Anyway—what would I do in Cornwall? And what about the children?

Penelope The idea was for just you and I to go, Nancy.

Nancy I couldn't possibly go without Melanie and Rupert. Whenever were you thinking of going?

Penelope (*rising*) It really doesn't *matter*.

Nancy It matters a lot. I have my life. (*She pulls her diary from her bag*) There's the church fête to be planned. The Conservative Conference—Melanie has all her Pony Club tests and there's camp—I promised Rupert I'd——

Penelope It doesn't matter.

Nancy I might be able to manage a couple of days later in the year—September perhaps——

Penelope It was just an idea, Nancy. It doesn't matter.

Noel appears from the garden

Noel (*mockingly*) Might I come in now, Mummy? My hand is no longer on fire.

Penelope Yes, do, Noel. I'm dying to hear what you're going to do with your share of the loot.

Noel gives Nancy a puzzled look

Nancy Mother's thinking of selling the panels.

Penelope Nancy is thinking of me selling the panels. And I'm thinking about what you'd all do with the money.

Nancy I'd spend it on the children, of course.

Noel Of course you would, diddums. But only after restoring that draughty old barn you live in.

Nancy It is not a draughty old barn. It happens to be a Grade 2 Listed Rectory.

Noel I think I'd probably set up on my own, Ma. With that sort of loot. Set myself up in business. Commodity broking probably.

Penelope Commodity broking indeed. Why not just go out and put it all on a horse? You should be ashamed of yourself. You don't give two hoots about anything or anybody except yourself—and money. You know, up until now I never thought once about selling the panels—but since you've brought the matter up if I do choose to sell them—which well I may—I think I might keep every penny for myself. Do stop looking so shocked—the panels are mine and therefore so would the money. Mine to do as I liked with. To blow it all on an around the world cruise if I felt so disposed.

Noel Hang on. Hang on a minute, Ma—I think you and I should discuss these things. After all, I am your son.

Penelope Discuss what? The fact that you want to get your hands on some money *now*? Really, Noel—sometimes you're so like your father——

Noel I am only trying to help, Ma. I am only trying to help you *financially*.

Penelope Oh, of course you're not, Noel! You're trying to help *yourself* financially. It's my money and so I can do exactly what I like with it.

Noel That's not a very responsible attitude if I may say so, Ma.

Nancy Responsibility is hardly Mother's strongest suit if you remember, Noel.

Penelope (*amazed*) I *beg* your pardon, Nancy?

Nancy (*wide-eyed*) I'm only echoing what Granny Keeling used to say. Granny Keeling always used to say——

Penelope What is the *matter* with you two, anyway? Until you were grown up, you two—you three—the three of you were all that mattered in my life. You *were* my life. But now—now——

Noel (*chipping in*) Yes? Now? Now what?

Penelope (*anguished*) Noel. Noel you are my son. Don't you understand? You are my son. And if I didn't love you so much——

Noel No—no, I don't understand as it happens. If I'm the son you love so much then you should take me into your confidence—and discuss these things with me.

Nancy Noel's absolutely right, Mother. You really don't take any of us into your confidence. At least certainly not George and me. Me least of all. I really have tried my best, you know. To be the sort of daughter you wanted me to be. To be a good wife and mother—to educate my children—your grandchildren—to educate them properly—the way you would like them to be educated——

Penelope Now Nancy—Nancy, before you go any further——

Nancy No, just hear me out, Mother, please? Because while we are on the subject of education, here is a perfect example of how you could make your money work to its best—to its best … you know…

Penelope We have been through this, Nancy—and this is your business, not mine. Please remember it was yours and George's decision to send your children to these absurdly expensive private schools and no-one else's.

Nancy We are not talking about where we choose to educate our children, Mother—which incidentally is really none of your business——

Penelope Really? They're my grandchildren.

Nancy Nominally perhaps. You show more interest in your garden than you do in your grandchildren. You never come and see them. You never ask them here—you hardly ever come to see us as a matter of fact—no matter how often we ask you——

Noel (*sighing*) Shut up about your bloody children. Your bloody children are neither here nor there.

Nancy They're worth a great deal more financial support than you are! With your get-rich-quick crackpot schemes! You really would squander any inheritance! You'd just simply gamble it away, Noel——

Olivia appears from the garden during the following

Noel I'd rather do that any day and end up destitute! Than live in a society full of people like you—and George—and your simply appalling kids!

Olivia I thought I heard the familiar sounds of a family discussion.

Penelope Will you stop it? The both of you? You are to stop this *at once*. You have no right to behave like this—none whatsoever. All this because you think I might be deciding to sell something that for some reason you imagine by rights belongs to you? I'm ashamed of you. Of both of you.

Nancy I've had quite enough. (*She collects her belongings*) I really don't need this. I really don't. (*She calls off*) George?

Noel (*mimicking her*) George? Walkies!

Penelope I think it's time you went as well, Noel. You've both behaved dreadfully.

Olivia (*with a glare at Noel*) I'm going to make a start on the washing up.

Noel Goody two shoes.

Olivia Careful, Noel. You don't want me for an enemy.

Penelope Leave it, Olivia—I can manage.

Nancy Why do you have to do it? You've got a slave.

Penelope You had better not be referring to Antonia, Nancy. Antonia is here because I asked her to come here. As my guest.

Penelope exits

Noel Well done, Sis. That was the clincher.

Nancy What about you? Big mouth.

Noel Charming.

Olivia Neither of you deserve Mumma. Do you know that? Neither one of you.

Nancy And of course you do.

Olivia At least I haven't just done what you two have done. Hurt the best person you'll ever know.

Nancy and Noel leave

Olivia watches them go. Then she turns to go and help her mother, but Penelope has reappeared, doing up her apron

Take that off, Mumma. I'll do the washing up. You come and sit down.
Penelope I'm perfectly well enough to do the washing up.
Olivia Then we'll do it together. (*About to lead Penelope off*)
Penelope (*stopping*) Could you come to Cornwall with me, Olivia?
Olivia Cornwall, Mumma? (*She smiles*) When?
Penelope As soon as possible. I know you're very busy.
Olivia (*stalling*) No—what a *lovely* idea! Cornwall? What—just you and I?
Penelope Nancy and Noel have better things to do apparently. I wanted us *all* to go. But they're too busy.
Olivia Well, I'm not—so you can count me in. I can't think of anything I'd like more.
Penelope (*genuinely delighted*) I knew *you* wouldn't let me down. I'd really like to go sometime this month. Ideally.
Olivia You're on. Blow work—Porthkerris here we come!

They embrace, Olivia kissing her mother warmly. They look at each other and Olivia smiles

That is a date. And I mean it.
Penelope (*smiling*) Good. I'm so glad.
Olivia I can't think of anything nicer. Now—now I'm going to do the washing up——
Penelope (*resisting*) No, you're not——
Olivia (*insisting, pushing her mother towards the straw armchair*) Yes, I am—while you sit and take the weight off your feet—and dream about Cornwall. You've done enough already.
Penelope I am a little tired…
Olivia Hardly surprising. Now you just crash out in your favourite old chair—and have forty winks. I can manage.

Olivia settles her mother in her chair

Penelope I meant to say how nice you look. Is that a new dress?
Olivia Bought it in the sales.
Penelope Thought I hadn't seen you in it.

Having got her mother settled, Olivia kisses the top of her head then exits through the little conservatory

(*To herself*) I thought it was a new dress. Nothing like a nice, new dress…
(*She begins to recollect*)

The Lights dim slightly above Penelope as they come up on the area DS *at which Penelope stares in her daydream*

In the new Light is seen the figure of Penny, in stockings and a slip, standing in front of a cheval mirror

There is a chair nearby with a dress still in its tissue paper folded over the back. She stands looking at herself, as if seeing herself as a woman for the first time in a long time. Then she unwraps the dress from its tissues, slips it over her head, does up the buttons and then the wide belt. The dress is plain red with a square neck, padded shoulders and a skirt of flaring pleats. She turns in front of the mirror to admire herself

Lawrence enters and sees Penny. He stops and looks at her

Lawrence Hallo—that new?
Penny What do you think?
Lawrence Poppy red. My favourite. Especially on you. Sophie's colour too. Poppy or Venetian. Another drinks party?
Penny (*brushing her hair*) No. (*She glances at her father*) I've been asked out to dinner. By Richard.

Lawrence goes to look as if out of a window

Lawrence Good.
Penny You think I should go?
Lawrence You know perfectly well what I think, Pen.
Penny Supposing...
Lawrence (*widening his eyes*) Supposing...

Silence as she looks at him then she smiles

Penny You're dreadful, Papa. You know that.
Lawrence Appalling. Beyond redemption.
Penny (*kisssing him*) We've always been able to talk, haven't we? (*She leans forward and kisses him again, gently on the cheek*)
Lawrence I wouldn't still be here if it wasn't for you. As for what you do— your mind is your own. You're old enough to make your own decisions.
Penny I know. And I have. (*She smiles at him, then turns round again so that he may see the full effect of her dress*)

Lawrence smiles. A doorbell rings, but they don't hear it. Neither does Penelope who still stares into space. The Lights go down on Penny and Lawrence and up on Penelope as voices are heard off

Brookner (*off*) What a perfectly lovely spot. How I love the Cotswolds.
Ellen (*off*) You do say Mrs Keeling was expecting you, sir? It's just that...
Brookner (*off*) She should be. Unless I've got the wrong day—which I don't
think I have...

Ellen appears at the side of the conservatory

Ellen It's just that—— (*Seeing the unmoving back of Penelope in the chair
for a moment, She thinks the worst. She stops in her tracks*)

If you'll just excuse me for a moment, sir—if you wouldn't mind waiting
here——

*Brookner has followed her in. He is a distinguished-looking man,
immaculately dressed and carrying an expensive, old-fashioned lawyer's
briefcase*

Brookner Not at all. Not at all—what a charming little gazebo. Quite
charming.
Ellen Won't keep you a minute, sir.
Brookner And what a perfectly lovely garden.

*Leaving the visitor behind, Ellen hurries to Penelope's side. She hesitates,
then puts a hand on Penelope's shoulder. Penelope's eyes are open*

Ellen Mrs Keeling?

Silence

Mrs Keeling——

*Penelope suddenly wakes with a start. She stares in front of herself, a little
disorientated. Ellen practically gasps out loud, but manages to control her
relief*

Penelope Gracious heavens—I was miles away.
Ellen You have a visitor, Mrs Keeling.
Penelope I was dreaming—dreaming of—what *was* I dreaming of?
Ellen (*with a glance backwards*) A Mr Brookner. (*She hands Penelope a
card*)

Penelope comes to

Penelope Mr Brookner? Oh, heavens above, Ellen! I'd—I thought he wasn't coming till tomorrow.

Ellen I wondered why you didn't say nothing. He's waiting outside.

Penelope (*flapping*) Oh, for heaven's sake, Ellen—show the poor man in at once. (*She stands, tidying herself as best she may*)

Ellen goes to admit Brookner

Ellen Mr Brookner, Mrs Keeling.

Ellen exits

Penelope Mr Brookner. Forgive me—I was on the telephone—wretched instrument. It always rings at the wrong time.

Brookner Mine has exactly the same habit. How do you do. (*He shakes her hand and looks round*) What a charming house you have. And such a beautiful garden.

Penelope We're gradually getting it back in shape. Got a little out of hand last year.

Brookner Something else we have in common. My garden does exactly the same thing. How long have you lived here now?

Penelope Over six years. Nearly seven.

Brookner It really is charming.

Penelope I'm very lucky. Would you like some coffee? I forgot to ask Ellen... (*She goes to call Ellen*) I'm quite at sixes and sevens today. Ellen?

But Brookner by now has found the painting of The Shell Seekers *and stands* DC *in front of the fireplace, looking up at the work in silence*

I can't imagine what I was thinking. You did say you wanted coffee?

Brookner (*not turning back*) That would be very nice, thank you.

Penelope (*calling*) Ellen dear? I forgot to ask you to make some coffee! Please!

Ellen (*off*) I'll put the kettle on right away, Mrs K!

Penelope Ellen's what used to be called a treasure. Which I'm sure is quite politically incorrect now—but who cares. (*She walks up behind Brookner*) She is a treasure and I'd be quite lost without her.

Brookner Good heavens. (*He turns*) Forgive me. I'm so sorry but... (*Beat*) This—this painting. I'd heard rumours of its existence of course——

Penelope My—you are a serious Lawrence Stern fan. Yes—that's *The Shell Seekers*. Pappa painted it in 1927 and other than for a short loan to his local gallery during the war it's never been shown. (*She looks up at the painting*) It was my father's last work. He gave it to me as a wedding present. I wanted you to see it, not because I'm selling it because I'm not—I would never ever sell this painting—no, I wanted you to see it because it puts his work into the proper perspective.

Brookner I see. Because your father has certainly always been seen purely as Pre-Raphaelite and Post Pre-Raphaelite.

Penelope This is the direction in which he *really* wanted to go. What stopped him was his arthritis. It was already affecting him badly when he painted this.

Brookner It really is superb. And I'm very grateful to you for letting me see it. (*He turns to her*)

Penelope (*deciding*) Good. Now let me show you the panels. Since the coffee is still on its way. (*She leads the way*) As I told you on the telephone, they are unfinished. Again—due to my father's arthritis. By the time he got round to thinking about finishing them he could no longer hold his brushes.

The phone rings. Hearing it, Penelope hesitates

See what I mean about the telephone?

Brookner (*sighing*) As I said—mine's just the same.

Penelope The panels are at the top of the stairs. So why don't you go on up? You can't miss them. I really had better answer this—if you'll excuse me.

Brookner At the top of the stairs?

Penelope You can't miss them.

Brookner goes off and up the stairs

Penelope crosses to a small table with the phone and answers it as Olivia appears in a Light DS from her, waiting on the other end of the line. Olivia is checking a galley proof one-handed

Olivia Mumma?

Penelope Olivia. (*She glances round*) Do you think I could call you back, darling? There's someone here—it's not very convenient.

Olivia I only want a quick word, Mumma—won't take a minute. It's about—it's about Cornwall—I was wondering if we could perhaps move it forward to next month—I know you've made all the arrangements but——

Penelope (*sighing*) But it's all mapped out, Olivia. The whole idea of the trip is so that we could——

Olivia (*closing her eyes*) I know, Mumma, I know—but I really can't help it when the management suddenly spin me something right out of the blue. They say I simply *have* to go to Paris for the Collections.

Penelope You must have known about the Collections. They always come round the same time of year. And you always have to go.

Olivia (*biting her lip*) I thought I'd be able to sidestep them this year. By sending my assistant—but the management *insist*.

Penelope (*wearily*) I see. And work comes first.

Olivia I would *far* prefer to come with you to Cornwall, Mumma! Infinitely! I was so looking forward to it. If it was down to me, Mumma——

Penelope I know, Olivia, I know. You have a nice time in Paris—and we'll meet and have lunch or something when I get back.

Olivia (*puzzled*) You're surely not going by yourself?

Penelope If I have to. I told you. This is the only time I can go. Bye, darling—take care. (*She puts the phone down on her*)

Olivia (*perplexed*) Mumma?

But the phone is dead. Olivia stands brooding. Then she dials a fresh number

Hank? Hank, sweetie—it's me—'Livia. And it's OK—guess what? I've cleared it. I can come with you to Antigua after all—yes, I'm glad too. I can't wait in fact. Bye, darling. Bye.

The Lights fade on Olivia. Penelope turns back, her face deeply frowning. She is dreadfully wounded by Olivia finally letting her down, but of course will do her best not to show it

Her reverie is interrupted by Roy Brookner coming down the stairs

Penelope looks to him

Brookner Well, they're wonderful, Mrs Keeling. You say they're unfinished and I'm quite sure technically you're right—yet in a way they are marvellously complete. (*He comes into the room*)

Penelope follows after she has surreptitiously checked and taken a deep restorative breath

Penelope (*a little absently*) I'm so glad you liked them.

Brookner Of course they're not so finely detailed or as meticulous as the great works he executed at the turn of the century—but they're still perfect in their way. What a colourist he was. Quite superb.

Penelope (*recovered now, coming to his side*) My children—well, they've either ignored them. Or been scathing about them—but I've always loved them. They've given me infinite pleasure.

Brookner So they should, Mrs Keeling. Your father was a great painter. Now. Is that all you wanted me to see? You mentioned something about...

Penelope Yes, I did. But this is to go no further. For the moment this is just between you and me. You'll find a portfolio—just by the stairs. If you would be so kind as to fetch it?

Brookner Of course. (*He looks at her, then goes and collects a large artist's portfolio tied with black ribbon*)

Penelope gestures for him to open it

Penelope No—please.

Brookner sits with the portfolio on his knees for a moment. He looks at Penelope who smiles, encouraging him to continue. He does so, opening the portfolio, laying it on the floor in front of him

(*With a laugh*) The suspense——

Brookner stares at the contents of the folder on the floor at his feet. When he sees the sketches he frowns, and stops, staring in wonder at the first item. His hands hang between his knees as he looks, unable to move or comment. Then he glances at Penelope who has now become impassive

There are fourteen sketches altogether.

Carefully Brookner lifts the oil-painted sketches one by one, placing them on top of each other on one side of the open folder as he does so

Brookner Where did you—where have they been…
Penelope In a panel at the back of my wardrobe. They've been there for twenty-five years. Before that they were in my father's studio—in Oakley Street.
Brookner (*by now reverentially*) Does anyone else know of their existence?
Penelope No-one. I think my son suspects—judging from his interest in my attic—an interest that has now passed…
Brookner (*looking at her*) Are they insured?

She shakes her head

That why you hid them?
Penelope I didn't want my husband to find them. He was a gambler. I didn't know when I married him—well, it was wartime. Things look very different in wartime.
Brookner A uniform romance? There were plenty of those, of course.
Penelope I'm afraid that's exactly what it was. Anyway—once back in Civvy Street he got quite badly into debt—and I knew that he was quite capable of just taking the paintings my father had left me and selling them. So I sold some jewellery instead—which saw us over that particular crisis.

Until we were faced with our son's first set of school fees when I had to sell
our family cottage in Cornwall. Ever since when I've had this terrible
yearning to buy a little granite cottage back there, with a palm tree and a
view of the sea. But my children talked me out of it. Said I'd be in a dim
and distant land. My son-in-law found this place—which I was told was
a much more sensible option for someone in my position.

Brookner Meaning more sensible for people in their position.

Penelope (*smiling*) Which is how and why I shall end my life here in the
Cotswolds and not within sight and sound of the sea.

Brookner And your husband?

Penelope He left me. Ran off with his secretary. I know—as corny as that.
(*She smiles*) Now—the panels.

Brookner Is there any urgency? Because having just had our big sale of
Victorian paintings it'll be another six months at least.

Penelope I would rather prefer to sell them now. Couldn't you perhaps find
me a private buyer?

Brookner You might not get such a good price...

Penelope And there again I might.

Brookner (*thinking*) Hmm. There is this American—a Philadelphian to be
precise—he was the underbidder for *The Water Carriers* and I know he
wants a Stern. I shall make enquiries.

Penelope Good. Thank you.

Brookner As for the sketches—would you like me to give an indication as
to their possible value?

Penelope Yes, please.

Brookner Conservatively—upwards of ten thousand pounds each.

Penelope (*staring at him*) My mathematics are appalling.

Brookner We should be able to get you somewhere in the region of one
hundred and fifty to one hundred and eighty thousand pounds.

Penelope (*smiling and nodding to herself*) That would make my father very
happy, Mr Brookner. He always used to say that the greatest gift a parent
can leave a child is that parent's independence.

Brookner Your father sounds as if he was a bit of a philosopher as well.

*Penelope suddenly frowns, as if distracted by something. Brookner looks at
her suddenly a little anxiously*

Are you feeling all right, Mrs Keeling? You've rather lost colour——

Penelope (*slowly and quietly*) No—no, I'm fine, Mr Brookner—thank you.
No, it was really quite extraordinary. For a moment I could suddenly smell
my father's studio. The linseed oil—the turps—the varnish. The sea even.

Brookner (*still concerned about her*) Look—look, why don't you sit down
for a moment—here in the sunshine——

Penelope (*allowing herself to be led*) It was exactly as if I was there.
Brookner You just sit down while I go and chase up that coffee.

Having settled her in her straw chair, Brookner eases himself out to find
Ellen

Penelope is oblivious to all this, sitting peacefully and letting her memories
wash over her

Penelope It was exactly as if I was there. (*She closes her eyes, once again*
swept away with her memories)

The Lights fade leaving Penelope lit in a single spot as the sound of crashing
sea waves is heard and the call of circling gulls. Then us of where only
Penelope now stands there is the glow of a lit stove. Lights up on what
suggests the place to be Lawrence Stern's studio in Cornwall. It is evening,
with a dark sky, and just the sound of the wind and the seas

Two figures sit huddled getting warm, Penny in a thick white fisherman's
jersey and Richard in dark trousers and a black sweater

Penelope is now sidelined watching her past

Richard How long since your father worked here?
Penny I don't know. Years.
Richard It looks—and *smells*—as if he never stopped. I love the smell of
painters' studios. Turps and linseed oil—oil paint and varnish.
Penny I've always thought this place was magic, ever since I was a child.
We always came here after surfing. Lit the stove. Made tea. Dunked
gingerbread biscuits and sat here swaddled in towels and thick woollen
blankets. Some years—if there'd been really bad storms in the winter, the
sand would be up to the window. But then at other times, other years it
would be like today. With a twenty foot drop. And you'd have to climb
down to the beach by rope ladder. Except you. You'd have scaled your way
down. Where did you learn to rock climb?
Richard In the Cairngorms. We've always been climbers, our family. When
the war's over I intend to do some really serious climbing.
Penny You see? That's the difference between you and me. You're always
looking ahead. And I'm always looking back.
Richard You do sometimes give the impression that your life ended the day
war broke out. You're too young to think like that.
Penny I think twenty-four's rather old.
Richard When's your birthday?

Penny It was last month. September. When you were away.
Richard   September.
          September has come, it is hers
          Whose vitality leaps in the autumn,
     (*Looking at her*) You familiar with Louis MacNeice?
Penny He's Papa's favourite poet.
Richard Then you must know the poem called *Autumn Journal*.
Penny Must I?
Richard It's very apt.
Penny Say it to me.
Richard Right. Right...
          September has come, it is hers
          Whose vitality leaps in the autumn,
          Whose nature prefers—
          Whose nature prefers... (*His voice fades off*)
Penelope (*picking it up*) Whose nature prefers
          Trees without leaves and a fire in the fireplace.
          So I give her this month and the next
          Though the whole of my year should be hers who has rendered
               already
          So many of its days intolerable or perplexed
          But so many more so happy.
          Who has left a scent on my life, and left my walls
          Dancing over and over with her shadow
          Whose hair is twined in all my waterfalls
Penelope & Richard And all of London littered with remembered kisses.
Penny Is that me? Is that how you see me? Rendering your days intolerable?
     And perplexed?
Richard I see you as leaving a scent on my life, and my walls dancing over
     and over with your shadow. And your hair entwined in all my waterfalls.
Penny And all of Cornwall littered with remembered kisses.

He leans over to her and they kiss again, longer

Richard You know I love you, Penny. I've been in love with you from that
     first moment when I was introduced to you. Down by the quay. And you
     stood there with your hair blowing in the wind. Looking like a gypsy angel.
Penny (*slowly*) A gypsy angel.
Richard My gypsy angel.

*They kiss. The Lights fade—there is the sound of the sea below the studio,
magnified, then the sound of war, of guns, machine guns, rifles, big guns, the
sound of battle in other words until it reaches almost deafening proportion*

Fade the sound of battle as the Lights come up on Roy Brookner standing
DC, *dressed differently, looking up at the invisible* Shell Seekers *above the*
fireplace

Ellen comes on with a glass of whisky on a tray. She hands it to Brookner

Ellen Mrs Keeling won't keep you. She didn't have a very good night.
Brookner (*anxiously*) I do hope she's all right. I thought she didn't look all
that well last time I was here.
Ellen (*looking back at him*) Hardly surprising. She's not that long out of
hospital.
Brookner I see. How is she now?
Ellen You ask me. She's better than she was, but to be quite honest, Mr
Brookner, I could tell you more about the Sphinx than Mrs K sometimes.
Brookner Perhaps I should go. I only dropped in because I was staying in
the neighbourhood——

Penelope enters with a glass in her hand

Penelope I'm so sorry to have kept you waiting, Mr Brookner.
Brookner You haven't kept me waiting at all. Being in the neighbour–
hood——
Penelope I hate keeping people waiting—and you will stay to lunch, won't
you? I meant to ask you on the telephone, but it clean went out of my head.
It will be no trouble—I do assure you. Ellen here's done the cooking today.
Brookner If you're sure it won't be an imposition. Something certainly
smells delicious.
Penelope Ellen's steak and kidney pie. Best in the world. Thank you, Ellen.

Ellen exits, leaving Penelope and Roy Brookner in front of the invisible
painting

Brookner If Thomas Werner the Third knew of *The Shell Seeker*s'
existence——
Penelope It wouldn't make the slightest difference—because it's still not for
sale. So you're at The Old Rectory. Staying with the Hacketts. They have
some very interesting paintings. Very keen on the mid-wars English
school. I'm so glad you called.
Brookner I'm glad, too. I wanted to see you again.

Penelope gives him a look of a different nature, then smiles at him

Penelope Are you married, Mr Brookner?

Brookner Happily—no, Mrs Keeling. Unhappily—yes.
Penelope Should I laugh?
Brookner Beats crying.

Penelope laughs. She takes a sip of her drink, then sits

We're getting divorced. Seems silly perhaps—at this age—but there you
are. The wheels can come off at any age I suppose.
Penelope It's no fun. Getting divorced. Whatever they tell you. You still end
up feeling like a failure, particularly when your husband runs off with a
younger woman. My husband was terribly good looking, you know. Quite
dashing in fact—and very plausible. But we should never have got
married. That was my fault.
Brookner Were you married long?
Penelope How long's too long? I couldn't leave the children. And he
couldn't really settle into Civvy Street. But I really should have given it
more thought. My father always used to say go and have a damn good look
at their mothers before you marry 'em. My husband's mother was an
absolute shocker.

Brookner laughs then finishes his drink

Now. Bring me up to date with your news.
Brookner Well. Mr Werner the Third is a great admirer of your father's. And
he's offered two hundred thousand for the panels.

Penelope's eyes open wide

And being American he'd like an answer by tomorrow.
Penelope I don't think we can possibly say no to two hundred thousand
pounds. Do you, Mr Brookner?
Brookner I don't think we can. And please call me Roy.
Penelope And you call me Penelope. I've been saving a rather good bottle
of wine for such an occasion—it's a Chateau Latour or something rather
grand.
Brookner If you're sure.
Penelope I've never been surer. And over lunch I want to talk to you about
The Shell Seekers.

*Brookner frowns at her but Penelope just smiles and raises her glass. He
raises his back to her. Fade to black*

Lights up on another area, the café as in Act I where Nancy and Olivia are once more having lunch

Nancy She's doing *what*?
Olivia You heard, Nancy. Otherwise you wouldn't be so outraged.
Nancy She is being taken for a ride by those two. You mark my words. If ever I saw two people on the make—it's them.
Olivia All they're doing is going to Cornwall with her. Which none of us could be bothered to do.
Nancy Have you any idea what a week at *The Sands* costs? For three?
Olivia Mumma can afford it. (*She smiles to herself*) An American millionaire has just bought the panels. For two hundred thousand pounds.
Nancy (*aghast*) *What?*
Olivia I told you last time we had lunch.
Nancy They can't be worth that sort of money. Two unfinished panels? They can't be worth *two hundred thousand pounds*.
Olivia You should be delighted—you and Noel. After all, you were nagging her to sell.
Nancy She told you, did she?
Olivia She wrote to me. She was very upset. You really had no right to set about her like that.
Nancy What's she going to do with the money? Did she tell you that as well?
Olivia Keep it. And spend it. And good for her. And there's something else you ought to know. (*She pauses*) She's given *The Shell Seekers* away. She's donated it to Grandfather's Gallery in memory of Grandfather. Which is another reason for her trip.
Nancy No, this I don't believe.
Olivia She wants to go and look at it—hanging in its new home.
Nancy She can't have just *given* it away.
Olivia Well, she has.

Upstage, as the Lights come up slowly, Danus is seen setting up a beach chair for Penelope while Antonia and Penelope lay out a picnic

Nancy But it's worth—it's worth at *least* half a million pounds.
Olivia Possibly more now.
Nancy She always told us she couldn't live without *The Shell Seekers*.
Olivia Seems she's changed her mind. I wonder why. She says she wants to share it with other people. She wants other people to enjoy it.
Nancy What about us? We're her *family*!
Olivia She says all we have to do is pay the admission charge.
Nancy Wait till Noel hears about this.
Olivia He knows already. I rang him this morning.
Nancy Really? What did he say?

Olivia (*smiling*) I think you can imagine.

The Lights fade on Nancy and Olivia and sunshine comes up on the beach group. Penelope now sits looking happily out to sea while Antonia and Danus prepare to go swimming

Danus Fantastic spot.

Penelope First time I ever came here was when I was seven. Papa had bought this huge green Bentley—which he could not only start but drive—much to Mama's astonishment.

Danus Not one of those fabulous old Bentleys? With a hood? And straps on the bonnet? With the handbrake outside the driver's door?

Antonia (*opening her eyes wide*) Hey—for someone who doesn't drive...

Penelope As a matter of fact it was. Why?

Danus They're worth an absolute fortune now.

Penelope You have such an interest in cars yet you don't drive.

Danus There's a reason.

Penelope I'm sure there is.

Antonia So what is it?

Danus (*staring at her, then*) Because I can't.

Antonia You could learn.

Danus Sure.

Antonia I'm going for my swim—before the tide turns. Come on...

Danus I'll follow you down. I want to soak up a bit more sun.

Antonia (*shrugging, giving a glance at the two of them together*) OK.

Antonia exits

Penelope and Danus sit in silence for a moment

Danus (*returning to the Bentley*) So what did happen to the Bentley? As a matter of interest.

Penelope (*laughing*) You won't believe this. Particularly you. I gave it away.

Danus (*seriously*) You're joking. You are *joking*.

Penelope Danus—a car like that just wasn't practical then. There was petrol rationing. The wretched thing drank petrol. My husband was furious when he found out. He wouldn't speak to me for a week.

Danus Wouldn't speak to you? I'd have divorced you.

Penelope (*laughing*) Oh, surely not, Richard.

Danus Danus.

Penelope (*frowning*) I'm sorry? What did you say?

Danus You called me Richard.

Penelope (*looking at him*) I'm so sorry, Danus. Did I really? I must be—what do you say? I must be losing it.

Danus (*shrugging and smiling*) I don't look like a Richard, do I?
Penelope Yes. As a matter of fact—you do.

Penelope looks at Danus with such affection that he frowns and drops his eyes

It's extraordinary really, how much you look like—like a Richard. Do you remember how—well—how startled I was when I first saw you?

Danus nods

There was a very good reason.
Danus I reminded you of someone.
Penelope I thought you were someone. While Antonia... (*She falls silent looking after where Antonia has gone*) At certain times—the set of her mouth—her eyes—even the way she walks. Most of all her attitude. At certain times...
Danus Yes? At certain times what?
Penelope (*smiling*) At certain times she's exactly like someone I knew. Someone I knew a long time ago. A very long time ago. (*Her smile fades as suddenly she remembers the pain, staring down to the unseen strand beneath them*)

The Lights fade, isolating Penelope with Danus falling into shadow

It was a day exactly like today. It was this time of year and it was a day just like today.

The sound of the sea increases, waves breaking on a shore, as sunlight now illuminates the DS area. There is the sound of a sea breeze and the cry of gulls

Penelope looks at the figure lit by the sunlight, Penny bent over the sand. She is shoeless, collecting sea shells in a bright red sand bucket

I was by myself down on the sands, collecting shells. I knew there was something wrong even before I saw him. I could feel it, suddenly in the air. It was as if someone had switched the sun off.

Her father Lawrence enters opposite her, dressed in a large Panama hat, old canvas trousers, cricket shirt and canvas beach shoes. He walks with a stick and is holding a letter

For a moment he stands and looks at his daughter who has looked up, not at him, but suddenly to frown at the sky above her as she slowly stands up

Lawrence I've been looking for you.

Penny (*seeing him and suddenly turning to face him*) Papa?

Lawrence I've been searching everywhere. Then I saw you from the studio——

Penny What is it, Papa? What's the matter? You wouldn't have come all the way down here unless... (*She sees the letter in her father's hand*) There's something wrong, isn't there?

Her father nods, barely. Penny buries her hands in her hair

It isn't Richard, is it? It is, isn't it? It's Richard.

Lawrence Oh, Penny. Penny, I'm so sorry, Pen——

Penny No. No, Papa——

Lawrence Richard's dead, Penny. I'm afraid Richard's been killed.

Penny stares at him

Somewhere they call—they call Omaha Beach... (*He holds out the letter hopelessly*)

Penny He can't have been. He can't have been killed.

Lawrence Bottom of the Cherbourg peninsula. Here. Letter's from his Colonel.

Penny (*staring at the letter*) Richard can't have been killed, Papa. It's not possible.

Lawrence Apparently Richard said if he—in the event of his... (*He is gathering his strength*)

Penny (*vehemently*) But Richard can't be dead!

Lawrence Achieved their objective apparently. Got to the top of the cliff— took the German gun battery. They did what they had to do before— before...

Penny stares blindly at the letter Lawrence still holds. Silence

Colonel Mellaby thought you might like to have this. (*He takes something else out of the envelope*)

Penny But he said he wouldn't be killed, Papa! He said he wouldn't be killed the last time we were together! He said it wouldn't happen! He promised me! He promised me he'd come back!

Lawrence (*handing her something*) Here. Here—it's a photograph.

Penny (*staring at the photograph*) Richard.

Lawrence Like—like my son, he was. Richard.

Penny Richard. (*She screws up the letter in her hand*)

Lawrence I loved him like a son. Like he was my own.

Penny (*almost inaudibly*) Oh, Richard... Richard...

Lawrence bows his head in grief. Penelope throws her head back and seemingly screams her grief—but in fact her anguish is silent and the scream is that of a seagull overhead, a cry that becomes hugely amplified, a cry joined by the screeching of many seagulls as Lawrence still stands, head bowed and Penny stands with her head thrown back in silent horror. The sounds of the gulls and the sea become muted as the Lights fade to black

The chatter of the gulls rises then fades as the Lights come back up on where Penelope sits with Danus at her feet

Penelope Papa died very soon after. Three weeks after in fact. Once Richard was gone...

Silence

It was just too much for him. It was too much for me—almost. But then I had Olivia.

Danus frowns at her but Penelope just shakes her head

Olivia isn't Richard's. No. I would love to have had a child by Richard— but it just didn't happen. Olivia was my consolation. I had her immediately after the war—and she's always been special ... because—because I suppose it was as though some physical part of Richard had stayed within me and become part of me. So that when Olivia was born it was as though something of Richard through me—became part of her.

Silence

I've never told anyone about this, you know. Not a soul. Not even told Olivia. I don't want you to tell anyone either.
Danus I promise.
Penelope You may tell Antonia. But not now. One day. Not now. You probably want to tell her now—but I'd rather you waited.
Danus (*after a pause*) What about your husband? I mean did he or didn't he—you know...
Penelope Ambrose?

She sees Danus half-smiling

Ambrose was quite a fashionable name then. There was even a famous band leader called *Ambrose*. But my Ambrose—no, he never knew—and he certainly never suspected anything. He wouldn't have.

Danus What was he like? What did he look like? Was he good-looking?

Penelope Oh, very. But as to what he was like... (*Wryly*) Well, you've met Noel—and you have met Nancy. So you've met my husband. Our marriage was an unmitigated disaster—and the disaster was entirely my fault. If Richard had survived, I would have left Ambrose like a shot and married Richard. As it was, Ambrose and I hardly saw a thing of each other during the war. So that when he came home, it was even worse. It was like being married to a stranger. Same thing happened to thousands of men and women. You learned to cope—then suddenly this strange man comes home—telling you what to do and what not. Ambrose was pretty awful anyway. He was a snob, a wastrel, a gambler, a womanizer—he really was awful. I'm afraid the only reason I married Ambrose was to get out of the Wrens.

Danus You said you joined up because you felt so strongly about the war.

Penelope I did. But I hated the Wrens and the Wrens didn't much like me. I was also absurdly homesick. So I ducked out. I was pregnant, I got married and I ducked out. I'm not very proud of it, but there you are. That's how and why I married Ambrose.

Danus OK—OK, so if we're telling secrets——

Penelope Yes? I can't believe you have a secret.

Danus It's about why I don't drive. And why I don't drink.

Penelope (*prompting him*) I'm listening.

Danus It's about something that happened a couple of years ago. Something not very good.

Lights down, Penelope and Darius exit. Lights up on Nancy and George as if out walking their dogs, Nancy in quilted coat carrying one lead, George likewise. They are walking DL *to* L

Nancy There is definitely something not quite right about that young man. Quite definitely. (*She calls*) And Nero! Nero don't you dare roll in that, you filthy dog!

George Don't be silly, Nancy. That's the sort of thing dogs do.

Nancy How that young man persuaded Mother to take Antonia and him away with her God only knows. (*She shakes her head*) And can't you stop your dog doing that!

George (*feebly*) Nero? Nero—don't do that—there's a good boy!

Nancy According to Olivia apparently *The Shell Seekers* looks wonderful in its new home. Isn't that lovely? (*Timing it*) But most of all guess *what*, George. Mother has only given that brat Antonia her Aunt Ethel's earrings.

George (*not really attending—as usual, but stopping*) Sorry? That significant?

Nancy Significant, George? *Aunt Ethel's earrings are Melanie's!*

George Sorry? How can Aunt Ethel's earrings possibly be Melanie's, Nancy?

Nancy (*seething*) Because Mother *promised them to Melanie, George!* And
have you no control over your wretched dog? Nero! (*She moves to exit*)
Nero! Will you put that poor little dog down, Nero!

Nancy exits, with George following

George Best do as she says, Nero… (*With a sniff*) If you know what's good
for you.

*Lights down on them and Lights up on the stage area now containing the
conservatory which brings the action back to Penelope's house in the
Cotswolds*

*Danus comes in, carrying some holiday luggage, as a taxi is heard
disappearing*

*Antonia comes out from the house through the conservatory with a can of
Coke*

Danus Penelope OK?
Antonia She's upstairs. She's just a bit tired from the journey.
Danus It was quite a haul.
Antonia (*looking round*) Hot, too.
Danus (*putting the cases down and looking round*) Garden could do with a
drink.
Antonia Here. Imagine you could as well. (*She hands him the can of Coke*)
Talking of gardens—I can't get Mannacan out of my head.
Danus Be some garden when it's finished! (*He puts the bags inside the
house*)
Antonia Right. (*She calls after him*) Sort of work you'd like to do!
Danus (*reappearing*) Like I said—if I had the capital.
Antonia Like I said how much exactly——
Danus (*frowning at her*) We've been through this, Antonia.
Antonia We haven't been through how much these earrings are worth. That
Penelope's just given me.
Danus (*angrily*) Don't even think about it. (*He turns his back on her*)
Antonia I didn't want to take them, Danus. Penelope insisted. And you mean
you don't know why?
Danus (*tightly*) No. I don't have an idea.
Antonia Oh, come *on. Come on.*

*Danus looks at her looking at him, seeing the look in her eyes, seeing how
pretty she is*

Danus You wouldn't really sell them to help me. Would you?

Antonia nods. Danus frowns

(*After a silence*) God. You really want part of this?
Antonia I'd like more than a part of it.

Danus stares at her hard then glances as it were up at the house

Danus OK—OK, but there are a few things you ought to know first—before we go any further.

Silence. Danus takes her hand and sits her on the garden bench behind them

You should know why I don't drink. Or drive. (*He hesitates, silent*) I've been meaning to tell you. It's because I'm an epileptic.

Antonia stares at him

Seriously. (*He breathes in and out deeply*) When I was in America, working on this ranch, one day I just blacked out. Cold. I'd felt a bit weird the day before—but I hadn't a clue anything might be wrong with me. Someone who was on the spot said he thought I might have had a fit—so they sent me to the local doctor who did some tests and he said I had epilepsy.
Antonia How could he be sure?
Danus Well... (*He shrugs*) He gave me a pretty thorough examination. Went right through my past history—and finally put it down to a kick I got on the head playing rugby.
Antonia So what happened when you got back to England? What did your parents say?
Danus I didn't tell them.

Antonia is amazed

(*Before she can interrupt*) Look. I had my reasons. I told you about my brother, remember? About him dying from meningitis only two years before. I really didn't think my parents could take any more worry. (*He shrugs*) I signed on with a new doctor—not the family one—he put me on some different dope—stuff I'm on now and—well. That's it. End of story.
Antonia I don't understand. You can't be serious. End of story? Have you ever had a reoccurrence? Another attack?
Danus Antonia——

Antonia I mean surely you've been examined here? You must have had a
second opinion?
Danus Antonia—I've been *diagnosed.*
Antonia I know. This is because of your parents, right? Because of your
brother?
Danus What do you know? You can't have any idea.
Antonia (*edgily*) I can have a slight idea.
Danus Not about this you can't. (*He moves to exit*)
Antonia Danus—where are you going?
Danus I'm going to get the hose.
Antonia Danus...? (*She makes to go after him*)
Danus Later. OK? Not now, Antonia—later.

Danus exits, leaving Antonia alone

*She watches him go with a worried frown, then sighs and retires to sit back
on the bench*

*Unseen by her Penelope has appeared at the doors of her conservatory and
is watching*

Penelope (*after a moment*) Antonia?
Antonia (*startled*) Penelope? Sorry—I didn't see you.
Penelope Are you all right, darling? (*She comes over to the bench*)
Antonia Not really. (*She looks at her*) Danus isn't very well.
Penelope I know. He told me.

Antonia looks round in astonishment

It isn't the end of the world, Antonia. And you mustn't be frightened. Even
if Danus does suffer from epilepsy, it's not exactly the end of the world.
Antonia What do you mean—even?
Penelope He really ought to have a second opinion. In fact my advice is that
he should tell his mother, and his father if necessary—and get them to send
him quick as poss. to a top neurosurgeon.
Antonia OK. And suppose they do—and suppose they find the doctor in
America was right after all.
Penelope That's a bridge you cross when you come to it, darling. (*She stops
and looks at her*) There are all sorts of treatments and drugs for *petit mal*
today. And there will be even better ones tomorrow. So if you're worried
about coping—don't be. You don't need to be. Not if you love him.
Antonia (*after a beat*) No. No, you're right. You're absolutely right. And I
do. I do love him, Penelope.

Penelope That's the main thing, Antonia dear. If you love one another. That's all that really counts. I promise.

Antonia looks at Penelope shyly then going close to her gently puts her arms round her. Penelope smiles over her shoulder and embraces her back. Penelope faces out front, so the look on her face is there to be seen. The sound of birdsong increases as the Lights fade down to black. Music—the single solo cello. Then above it a voice comes out of the dark—Olivia's voice

Olivia (*voice over*) Dearest Mumma. I'm sorry, I really am.

The Lights slowly come up again on Penelope who is now seated in her favourite old straw wing chair in the conservatory, her knees under a rug, and a warm cardigan around her shoulders even though it is a hot summer day. In her hands is a letter she is reading. After a moment she lowers the letter as her mind drifts into the immediate and not so immediate past. She starts to dream

Olivia now stands to one side of Penelope

I am so sorry I let you down.

Nancy appears

Nancy No, you *never* let her down, Olivia. *I'm* the one who always lets her down.

Olivia I should have gone to Cornwall with her. I really should have found a way.

Noel appears

Noel Ma, what on earth did you think you were doing? Giving away *The Shell Seekers*?

Nancy I do have a life, you know. I do happen to have a life of my own.

Noel *The Shell Seekers* was part of my inheritance!

Olivia I still say one of us should have gone to Cornwall with her.

Nancy So what was so wrong with you going? You were the one who *promised* to go.

Olivia I did my best. But they do throw these things at me with absolutely no notice at all.

Nancy I had a perfectly valid reason for not going.

Noel I had a perfectly valid reason for not going.

Olivia And I did everything I could to rearrange my diary.

Nancy Sometimes it's as if we weren't even her own children.
Olivia No, Nancy! How could you say that? That just isn't fair. It really isn't.
Nancy Oh, that's you all over. You've devoted your whole life to trying to keep on the right side of Mother.
Noel I feel just the same, Nancy. I have to say that sometimes it appears that I don't really matter.
Nancy (*sighing deeply*) As for me, I'm afraid I give up. I just give up.
Noel Seriously. Sometimes it's as if I simply don't matter one bit.
Olivia I'm just saying that one of us should have gone, that's all. Just one of us.
Nancy I had perfectly valid reasons. I have a life. I do happen to have a life of my own.

Nancy moves to exit

Noel I had perfectly valid reasons. Not that they count—because sometimes it seems I simply do not seem to matter.

Noel moves to exit

Olivia Well, I simply could not get out of going to Paris. I assure you—I did everything I could to rearrange my diary.

Olivia moves to exit

Nancy (*off; just an echo*) I give up... I really do...
Noel (*off; just an echo*) It was part of my *inheritance*, Ma...
Olivia (*off; just an echo*) I still say one of us should have gone with her...

Penelope wakes suddenly as if from a terrible nightmare

Penelope (*calling desperately*) Ellen! Ellen!
Ellen (*off*) Mrs K?

Ellen appears hurriedly

    Mrs K? (*She moves forward, quickly*) What ever is it, Mrs K——
Penelope Ellen?
Ellen It's only me. You all right?
Penelope (*so relieved*) Oh, Ellen. Ellen... (*She looks round her*) I must have been—I must have been dreaming.
Ellen (*fussing round her, tidying her rug*) There you are. You're all right now. It's all right now—I'm here. It's all right now.

Penelope I must have been dreaming. Nobody called, did they? (*She looks around her*) None of my children called, did they...?
Ellen (*shaking her head*) They all live a little far away, don't they? To be dropping in of a teatime. Tell you who did call though—ring rather...

Penelope looks round anxiously at her

Young Miss Antonia. Good news too... (*She plumps up the cushion behind Penelope's back*) Young Danus' initial results come through. From the people they sent him to see.
Penelope (*anxiously*) From the neurosurgeon? I wished you'd called me...
Ellen According to Miss Antonia apparently they can't get an absolutely accurate—you know...
Penelope Diagnosis?
Ellen Prognosis—until he's been off all medication for three months. But that everything they seen so far makes them think it mightn't be as bad as first thought. That he might not be an epileptic after all.
Penelope (*smiling at the malapropism*) Oh, thank God for that. That is wonderful news. Did Antonia say they have any idea what it might be? Or rather might have been?
Ellen They said something about plain common or garden heatstroke—least I think that's what Miss Antonia said.
Penelope I really would have liked to have spoken to Antonia, Ellen.
Ellen You can call her when you've had your tea. You can ask her then all about it. My auntie Doreen used to get heatstroke, you know. She was a martyr to it as it happens. Soon as the sun hit her, out she'd go. Out she'd go like a light.
Penelope I'm so relieved, Ellen. About Danus I mean. I can't tell you how happy that makes me.
Ellen You been worrying yourself sick about him, I know you have. (*Finally, she tucks the rug tight around Penelope's knees*)
Penelope I couldn't have borne it. If anything had stopped those two young people from getting together——
Ellen (*overlapping her*) You're a proper old fussbudget, aren't you. Always have been—always will. (*She stands behind her, pausing as she realizes what she has said*) Anyhow. You're to stop your worrying. It's not good for you—getting yourself all fluffed up.
Penelope I'm not in the least fluffed up, Ellen. Not now. Not now that there's a chance Richard will be all right.
Ellen Not now there's a chance who might be all right? You said Richard.
Penelope I didn't. Did I?
Ellen Clear as day. You called Danus Richard. Heard you clear as day.
Penelope (*smiling*) Names. You know what I'm like nowadays with names, Ellen. I meant—Danus.

Ellen I'll go and make us a nice cup of tea. That's what you need—a nice cup of tea.

Penelope Ellen? (*She catches her hand and holds it*) Ellen, I don't know what I would have done without you.

Ellen Driven some other poor old soul to distraction I'll be bound. (*She smiles behind her back*) I'll go and put that kettle on.

Penelope smiles and shakes her head

Penelope I mean it, Ellen. I don't know what I would have done without you.

Ellen So glad you had such a nice time in Cornwall. (*She makes to exit*)

Penelope sits thinking for a moment, her thoughts drifting

Penelope Oh, we did. We had such a lovely time.

Ellen (*going*) I really am so glad...

Ellen exits

Penelope (*distantly*) We had such a lovely time in Cornwall. (*She remembers*) It was just as it always was. It really was. It was just as if it was——

Penny appears DS, barefoot in a beach dress, a straw sun hat pushed on the back of her head. The white light turns to warm summer sunlight on her as she goes about her business of seeking out shells

Yesterday. (*She remembers*) And I'm bicycling. Freewheeling down between fuchsia hedges hung with pink and purple ballerinas. The road curves and is white and dusty. It feels like a Saturday feels—like Saturdays felt when you were young—and now I'm at Carn Cottage except it isn't Carn Cottage because it has a flat roof. Papa is here in his wide brimmed hat, painting. He doesn't have arthritis—he's painting big long bold strokes of colour on the canvas and now when I stand by him he doesn't look up—he just says *one day they will come—one day they will come to paint the warmth of the sun and the colour of the wind.* Now I'm looking over the edge of the roof and there's a garden, with a pool. It's just like Ibiza. Just like it was on Ibiza. Hot and clear. So clear. Mama is swimming in the pool—naked as ever. Just as she always swims. Her hair is wet and sleek—sleek as a seal's fur. I stand up on the roof to look at the view but I can see it isn't the bay—it's North Beach, and the tide is out—way, way out—in fact I can hardly see the sea—but I can see me. I'm down there on the sands, searching with a scarlet bucket full of huge shells. But I'm not searching for shells. I'm searching not for something—but for somebody.

Someone I know is nearby. As I do the wind blows in a mist off the sea—
curling over the beach like smoke——

*A faint fret from the sea blows in from the other side towards Penny, who
looks up*

And now I can see him. I can see him. He's walking towards me. He's in
uniform——

*The figure of a man, Richard, appears in the mist. He remains shrouded
but as the fret begins to clear it is apparent he is in military uniform, that
of a marine officer. He stands and looks at Penny*

And he says——
Richard I've been looking everywhere for you.
Penny (*standing slowly*) Richard?
Richard I've been looking everywhere for you. (*He puts his hands out and
crosses to her. He meets up with her opposite where he came in and has
taken both her hands in his*)
Penelope (*putting out her own hands*) Richard. Richard… (*She closes her
hands as if holding invisible ones, her face wreathed in a sudden smile*)

*Richard turns Penny away, lets go of one hand and leads her by the other
US and into the night*

*Penelope sits with a smile on her face, then as Richard and Penny vanish into
darkness her hands drop to her side, she gives a gasp as her head falls back
on her cushion, and she is gone*

*The voice of Vera Lynn is heard singing: "We'll Meet Again" as the stage
goes to black. The song continues, then when the Lights come up, the stage
is bare except for the now darkened conservatory US and one small table set
DS to one side, and another small table opposite*

*Everyone in the family who is to enter will bring on a chair with them if
needed. Olivia and Nancy enter first, dressed as if straight from the
funeral, setting down their chairs*

Nancy I still can't believe the choice of music.
Olivia It was Mumma's choice.

During the following, Noel enters, carrying a tray of drinks

Nancy What can she have been thinking? Vera *Lynn*? At a funeral? I have never *been* so mortified.

Noel laughs, sets the tray down on a table, and begins to pour a drink. Nancy glares at him

Noel I love the idea of you being mortified at someone else's funeral. I thought the service was OK really. The music—the readings. The lot.

Nancy (*giving him a wide-eyed look, then to Olivia*) And I'd still like to know what Antonia's doing here.

Olivia She's here because I asked her.

Nancy And her little friend?

Olivia I asked Danus as well.

Nancy I'd really love to know why. And where's this famous *appointed trustee*? Who's another of Mother's little dodges, no doubt.

Olivia I happen to think Mr Brookner was a very good choice of Mumma's.

Nancy Yes. Well, you would. So why wasn't he at the funeral?

George enters, bringing with him Roy Brookner

George Mr Brookner, one and all...

Brookner So sorry for being late—there was an accident on the motorway... (*He puts his case and belongings down on the table*)

George prepares to introduce everyone

I really am sorry if I've kept you all waiting. And I'm particularly sorry because it made me miss the funeral.

George Traffic gets worse by the day, doesn't it? I'll say. Anyway— anyway, allow me to introduce my wife, Nancy, Mr Brookner—and my sister-in-law Olivia—and my brother-in-law Noel... (*He goes to pour himself a drink*)

Noel (*shaking hands*) Obviously a pretty bad accident to make you this late.

Brookner (*shaking hands*) Obviously. Traffic was tailed back for three or four miles.

George May I offer you a drink, Mr Brookner?

Brookner (*still upset, shaking his head*) No, thank you. I'm quite sure you're anxious to get on with proceedings.

Olivia You do have time. We're still waiting for Danus and Antonia—and Ellen, of course. (*To Nancy*) Also in line with Mumma's wishes. Here she is now.

George takes his drink and moves away as Ellen comes in, in her coat and hat, followed by Danus and Antonia

Ellen So sorry everyone—we were having a quick wander round the garden. Looking grand it is too. Mrs K would be so pleased. I was just saying to young Mr Muirfield here what a good job he's done.

Nancy A matter of opinion.

Brookner How are you, Ellen?

Ellen Going along nicely, thank you, Mr Brookner. Well as can be expected. I've done some finger food, Miss Olivia. Would you like me to fetch it in now?

Olivia Lovely. But I think we'll eat after we've heard the will, Ellen.

Nancy I thought wills always had to be read in the presence of a solicitor?

Brookner Not necessarily. If the family are happy with an executor...

Noel We're happy. If it helps move things on...

Brookner I'm very glad to hear it, Mr Keeling. If there's any dispute of course, then you would need to call on a lawyer. However—if you are all agreed?

Nancy looks at Antonia and Danus. Olivia interposes

Olivia Of course. If Mumma was happy to entrust her affairs to you, then that's fine. I imagine this is the most recent draft of her will? The one she re-drew when she—when she was on holiday. When she... (*She pauses*) When she was down in Cornwall.

Brookner It is. It was all done correctly. The lawyers have a covering letter detailing and specifying all your late mother's wishes, witnessed and dated.

Nancy Shouldn't this gathering—strictly speaking that is—shouldn't it be confined just to immediate family?

George Put a sock in it, Nancy.

Nancy I *beg* your pardon, George?

George I said—put a sock in it. The people who are here are here because your mother wanted them here. They have every right to be here.

Noel Attaboy, George! (*He grins*) So do as your husband says, Nancy. Put a sock in it and not before time too.

They all take their places at the table. Brookner lays the will out before him. He puts on his glasses and prepares to read

As he does so, Penelope appears from US, unseen of course by the assembled

Brookner Good. If everyone is ready? Then I shall begin. (*He reads*) This is the last will and testament of Penelope Keeling of Podmore Thatch, Temple Pudley, Gloucestershire. Dated the 1st of April 1984 and lodged with Mr Enderby of Enderby, Layton and Enderby. I have asked my good friend Roy Brookner, whom I appointed as my Trustee, to read it to you because it isn't the most formal of wills—and I would far rather imagine you all gathered at Podmore than sitting in some bleak legal offices.

Nancy glances apprehensively to one side where Antonia and Danus are the only ones standing. Penelope goes to stand behind Ellen

(*Reading*) Mrs Ellen Metcalfe.

Penelope Ellen dear.

Brookner (*reading*) To Mrs Ellen Metcalfe I leave the sum of five thousand pounds, as a gift for all she did.

Penelope You always looked after me so well. And you became such a good and such a reliable friend.

Nancy Yes, but five thousand pounds?

Olivia (*quickly*) I don't think anyone can object to that. If anyone outside the family should be remembered, it surely should be Ellen.

Nancy I suppose so. (*She shrugs*) I suppose you're right.

Noel shoots his sister a sideways look. Nancy ignores him, giving Danus and Antonia another pointed look instead. Noel has produced a silver ballpoint pen, small pocket notebook and calculator in readiness

Brookner (*reading*) Next—the furniture. There's not much, but to stop you squabbling I leave Nancy the Regency sofa table—my old dressing table—Olivia my writing desk which as you know was Papa's—and Noel the dining table and chairs. As for all the smaller bits of furniture, and other bits and pieces—they are all itemized in a list at the end of the will, as is exactly to whom each thing goes.

Nancy (*leaning forward*) What about the jewellery? That hardly falls under——

Penelope (*overlapping*) If you're wondering about the jewellery, Nancy— there isn't any. Not worth speaking of. I sold all the good stuff years ago to pay your father's gambling debts—and Noel's school fees. As for Aunt Ethel's earrings, the only pieces left—as you know...

Brookner (*reading*) The earrings have already been gifted to Antonia.

Nancy (*standing*) But they were *Melanie's*!

Olivia (*pulling her back down*) They were Mumma's. She wrote to me about it.

Brookner I understand she also lodged a copy of the letter with Enderby, Layton and Enderby, in case of any argument.

Penelope I don't want there to be any arguments which is why I've taken care to make sure everything's been done properly. And why I've decided that this is much the best way.

Brookner (*reading*) Namely that everything else is to be sold and the capital divided between you.

Nancy and Noel exchange delighted looks. Noel readies his pocket calculator for action

(*Reading*) I therefore devise and bequeath all my estate, both real and personal, upon my trustees to sell, call in, and convert the same into money… (*He looks up*) That means the residue of the estate… (*Back to reading the will*) To convert the same into money: the house, its contents, any stocks and shares and whatever's in the bank—after probate has been declared and all the taxes and expenses met.

Penelope (*walking round them and surveying them*) You should get about two hundred and seventy-five thousand for this place, so I'm told. Probably about forty to fifty thousand for the contents. And I have about seventy-five thousand in my shares portfolio.

Noel whistles approvingly

Brookner (*reading*) And due to the sale of the panels, a little over two hundred thousand in the bank.

Noel By my reckoning, that's nearly two hundred thou each, girls. Not bad— not bad at all.

Brookner If you wouldn't mind? Thank you. (*He reads*) Now to the final bequest.

Noel There's more?

Penelope You were right, Noel. About the sketches. It's just a pity you didn't come clean, instead of sneaking around pretending to clear up my attic. Fire risk indeed. You wouldn't ever have found them there. They have been hidden in the back of my wardrobe for years.

Noel (*quietly*) Shit.

Brookner (*reading*) There are fourteen sketches in all.

Noel Shit shit shit a *brick*!

Brookner Please.

Nancy You don't know to whom she's left them yet.

Brookner (*as himself*) At the present time they're in my safekeeping at the Bond Street branch of Sotheby's. (*He reads*) These sketches are to be left—all fourteen of them…

Everyone leans forward, waiting

Penelope (*standing behind him and putting her hands on his shoulders*) To Danus.

Nancy (*on her feet*) To *Danus?*
Brookner (*reading*) To Danus Muirfield—of Mill Cottage, Sprake Farm——
Noel (*also on his feet*) To bloody *Danus?*
Penelope To keep or sell according to his personal wishes.
Danus Dear God. Good God.
Noel Our dear mother was barking bloody mad!
Danus (*quietly*) Good God.

Noel stands up, lighting a cigarette angrily, walking away. Penelope retreats to stand by one wall, watching, shaking her head a little sadly

Noel (*turning back*) I shall contest this. I mean it.
Nancy You bet we bloody well will.
Olivia We most certainly will not.
Noel Have you any idea what they're *worth*, Miss Goody Two-Shoes? *Upwards of one hundred and fifty thousand bloody pounds!*
Olivia Even so—we are not going to contest it.

Danus frowns deeply, looking at Antonia. She takes his hand

Noel To think they were here all the time. In the back of her bloody *wardrobe*.
Nancy Of course we must contest this, Olivia. Don't be so stupid. Mother was obviously not in her right mind. Leaving all that *money*… (*Through gritted teeth*) To her *gardener*. (*She eyes the two youngsters then turns to Olivia*) What did they do to her, anyway? How did they get such a hold over her? Those earrings were my daughter's! They were Melanie's *by right!* They are nothing to this family, Olivia! Neither of them! Do you hear me? They're a pair of interlopers! Bloody adventurers!
Olivia (*alarmed at her sister's outburst*) For goodness sake, Nancy——
Nancy Olivia! They are nothing but a pair of little scheming opportunists!
Olivia (*icily*) That is quite enough. Do you hear me? That is *quite*—enough. (*She confronts her family, rather in the style she must use at the head of her editorial table at the magazine*)

Noel and Nancy stare at her, never really before having witnessed her undoubted authority

You should be ashamed of yourselves. Mumma has been dead less than a week yet here you both are fighting over her belongings like a couple of starving jackasses. We've all been left far more than we ever deserved. You try taking these kids to court and I will see you in hell. And as for saying Mumma wasn't in her right mind, Nancy. If you think you deserve anything more than you now have, then you really have taken leave of your senses. You think about what Mumma did for us. Our childhood, the love she showered on us—while all the time our father was gambling away the little money they had. Even her death has left us well provided for—and what do we do? We squabble about a pair of earrings. About some paintings that aren't even ours. Which were Mumma's to give to whoever she liked. If she'd wanted Melanie to have the earrings, Nancy, she'd have given the damned things to her. And if she'd wanted you to have the oil sketches, Noel——

Noel (*holding his hands up*) OK—OK, Sis. I get the point.

Olivia Mumma made her own will. She did what she wanted to do—which is all that matters. And if we are to do anything for Mumma—then what we're going to do is let her have the last word.

Nancy stares at her sister as Noel slowly smiles, putting away his pocket calculator and notebook. George smiles and starts to clap

George Well done, Olivia. Jolly good.

Nancy Have you taken complete leave of your senses, George?

George On the contrary. I think I've just come to them.

Noel (*to Brookner*) OK—so is that it? That the entire will?

Brookner Not quite. No. Your mother has something personal to say to you all.

Everyone retakes their places. Penelope comes back into their midst

She added a personal statement at the end of her will. It's addressed to the three of you. To Nancy—Olivia—and Noel.

Penelope I want you all to know just one thing. Whatever else you may think, I just want you to know I love you. I love all three of you. And I hope that now—now that I'm gone, now you have this little bit of security—I hope that Nancy—instead of always wanting something more I hope you will realize that you already have far more than most people do—and Noel—Noel I do hope you finally realize that no-one ever put enough on a winning horse. No-one. As for you, Olivia—I hope that next time you really fall in love, you realize love is a blessing and not a career. And one little word to you two young ones, Antonia—and Danus. Thank you. Thank you for bringing the sunlight into an October garden. (*She pauses*) Oh, and Antonia—it's only small—but it's something I want *you* to have, Antonia. Don't worry, Nancy—it's not valuable. At least it wouldn't be to you. It's a book of mine, Antonia. Mr Brookner has it. I parcelled it up and sent it to him before we left for Cornwall. That's it. Goodbye. Goodbye.

Penelope stands facing them, her back to us, and blows them all one kiss. Then she walks through the midst of them, beyond the invisible walls of the house and out to her conservatory where she stands surveying her beloved garden. Brookner closes the will and puts it back in his briefcase. The Lights go down on the conservatory. Antonia looks at Brookner who smiles at her, and from his brief takes the wrapped volume of poetry. He hands it to her. After a glance at Danus, Antonia begins to open it

George (*rising*) I don't know about anyone else, but I know I could do some serious damage to some of the goodly Ellen here's prog. (*He makes to exit*)
Noel Good thinking, George. (*He goes after him*) I was just the same at school. After a beating, first thing I wanted to do was to eat.

Noel and George exit

Nancy who is now standing, pulls down her dress and flicks back her hair and goes to get a sight of a copy of the will from Brookner while Antonia who has unwrapped the book of poetry looks at the spine

Antonia The poems of Louis MacNeice.
Olivia A rather special edition, too. (*She takes the book and looks at it and then in it*) This is Grandfather's copy.
Antonia Any idea why she wanted me to have it?
Danus There's something stuck in a page there. (*He takes the book from Olivia*) It's a photograph. (*He looks at the page*) Marking a bit in a poem called *Autumn Journal*. (*He reads it*) September it is come——
Antonia September? My birthday's in September. (*She takes the book back from him*) Except Penelope she can't possibly have known...

Danus is now distracted by what he has found in the book. A photograph. He stares at it, hard. Olivia, at his shoulder now, looks at the photo as well, then takes it from him. She looks amazed, looking from the photo to Danus and back again

Olivia Good heavens above.
Antonia Sorry? You look as though you've seen a ghost, Olivia.
Olivia Perhaps that's because I have.

Antonia takes the photo and looks

Antonia God, if it wasn't for the uniform...
Olivia You're absolutely right.
Danus (*quickly*) Not if you look closely——
Antonia Come on—at first sight... (*She stares at the photograph*)

Danus tries to reclaim it—but Olivia is taking another look

Olivia I wonder who he was.

Danus (*taking the photo back*) Judging from the uniform—and the fact that it was in the book of MacNeice's poems—I'd imagine he was a friend of your Grandfather's.

Olivia Ah. (*She allows him the photo*) Yes. Yes, of course.

Antonia (*not happy with it*) Even so. I think it's weird. How much you look like——

Danus (*quickly*) Listen—listen why don't we go for a walk in the garden? There's something I want to tell you.

Antonia But——

Danus Seriously. It's *very* important. And who knows? I might even try to read you that poem. OK?

Antonia (*shrugging*) OK.

Danus takes Antonia's hand and leads her US *as if to the garden. They disappear into the darkness*

Olivia (*looking after them*) Bet you anything he's going to propose.

Nancy (*taking note for the first time*) The gardener? Well, he can certainly afford to now, can't he?

Brookner I think they make a most charming couple. Absolutely charming.

Olivia And I think perhaps we could all do with a drink. Would you like to do the honours, Mr Brookner?

Brookner Why of course. What can I get you?

Olivia There's some rather good brandy in the large decanter.

Nancy has detached herself from them, coming DS. *Olivia notices and follows her now as Brookner pours the drinks*

You all right?

Nancy I'm fine, thank you. I just need a moment.

Olivia I know. Of course.

Nancy I loved Mother, you know. I really did.

Olivia She loved you too, Nancy.

Nancy I just wish I'd told her. It's too late now. I don't think I ever got round to telling Mother that—that... (*She can't go on*) I don't think I told her once.

Olivia (*on her own track*) I don't actually know how Mumma managed it, Nancy. It certainly can't have been easy. Not having the children you'd perhaps dreamed of having.

Nancy Now you have completely lost me I'm afraid.

Olivia If you don't love your husband, Nancy, I don't see how your children can be the children you'd once dreamed of having.

Nancy I don't care. It doesn't really matter now. I just wish I'd told Mother how I ... how I... (*She stops and sighs*) I really should have told her.
Olivia You didn't have to tell her, Nancy. Mumma knew. You couldn't have done more. As long as you tried your best——
Nancy (*resolutely*) But I didn't, Olivia. I'm afraid I came up rather short.
Olivia (*again with a smile*) I did say as long as you tried.
Nancy I think I came up the shortest. Quite easily. Anyway... (*She dabs her nose*) Anyway, I'm sorry for always being such a pain.
Olivia And I'm sorry, too. For always being—for always being such a goody two shoes.

Which earns a look from Nancy

Tell you what—why don't we both stop being quite such terrible pains? Right? For Mumma.
Nancy (*after a moment's contemplation to make sure there isn't a catch somewhere*) Yes. All right—agreed. For Mother... (*She corrects herself*) For Mumma.

Brookner steps in and hands them their drinks. Nancy and Olivia regard each other then raise their glasses

Nancy |
           | (*together*) Mumma.
Olivia |
Brookner Your mother was an exceptional woman. Quite exceptional.
Olivia Thank you, Mr Brookner. And thank you very much for arranging all this.
Brookner Least I could do, believe me. I was very fond of your mother. Extremely fond in fact. To your mother. (*He raises his glass*)
Olivia To Mumma.
Nancy To Mumma.
Brookner Penelope...

As they raise their glasses and drink, the Lights come up on Danus and Antonia in the garden, and on Penelope in her straw chair, c, sitting quite still. Danus is reading the poem to Antonia. They could just as well be Richard and Penny

Danus   September has come, it is hers
                   Whose vitality leaps in the autumn,
                   Whose nature prefers
                   Trees without leaves and a fire in the fireplace. (*His voice
                       fades*)

Penelope (*picking it up as before*) So I give her this month and the next
　　　　　　Though the whole of my year should be hers who has rendered
　　　　　　　already
　　　　　　So many of its days intolerable or perplexed
　　　　　　But so many more so happy.
　　　　　　Who has left a scent on my life, and left my walls
　　　　　　Dancing over and over with her shadow—
　　　　　　Whose hair is twined in all my waterfalls
　　　　　　And all of London littered with remembered kisses.

Danus/Richard puts his hands on Antonia/Penny's waist

　　　　　　And all of London littered with remembered kisses.

*The young couple embrace while up comes the sound of the sea, the crashing
of its waves and the calling of the permanently hungry seagulls as slowly the
Light fades to darkness*

CURTAIN

FURNITURE AND PROPERTY LIST

Further dressing may be added at the director's discretion

ACT I

On stage: Armchair
Small table. *On it*: phone
Huge framed painting of *The Shell Seekers* painted on gauze
Small white conservatory/gazebo
Straw chair
Plant catalogue
Plants
Wisteria
Drinks
Garden bench

During light change on page 6:
Set: Easel
Paint table. *On it*: glasses, bottle of tonic water
Fisherman's net
Chair. *On it*: 2 surfboards, striped bathing towel
Wireless radio
Old canvases
Gin bottle under sand bucket

Before light change on page 9:
Set: Table
Chair
Perrier bottle
Glass
Menu
glass of gin and tonic

Before light change on page 12:
Set: Lemon tree in fruit
2 deck chairs
Suntan oil
Towel
Wine bottle
Glasses

Set: Before light change on page 27:
           Cherry tree in bloom

Set: Before light change on page 33:
           2 chairs
           Straight back chair
           Backgammon board game on table
           Whisky

Off stage: Small overnight case (**Penelope**)
           Larger suitcase, plastic carrier bag full of personal items (**Ellen**)
           Tea tray (**Ellen**)
           Secateurs (**Nancy**)
           Two large gin and tonics (**Nancy**)
           Daily Telegraph newspaper (**George**)
           Chocolate (**Penny**)
           Paperwork (**Olivia**)
           Book (**Penelope**)
           Phone (**Noel**)
           Full log basket (**Ellen**)
           Armful of daffodils (**Penelope**)
           Loft ladder (**Stage Management**)
           Newspaper (**George**)
           Suitcase (**Antonia**)
           Bucket, sandwich, khaki rucksack (**Danus**)
           Basket full of cut tulips (**Penelope**)
           Letter written on thin yellow paper (**Penelope**)

Personal: **Nancy:** galoshes, headscarf
           Olivia : designer glasses, sunglasses in coat pocket, lipstick, compact
              mirror
           Antonia: round straw hat
           Noel: phone, cigarette
           Ellen: wrist-watch (worn throughout)
           Penelope: wrist-watch, timer (worn throughout)
           Olivia: wrist-watch (worn throughout)
           Antonia: dark glasses
           George: cigarettes in pocket
           Lawrence: large black hat
           Richard: half bottle of whisky

ACT II

Set:	Large artist's portfolio tied with black ribbon
	Before light change on page 45:
Set:	Cheval mirror
	Chair with dress in tissue paper folded over the back
	During Black-out on page 55:
Set:	2 small tables

Off stage: Cigarette (**Noel**)
Bag containing diary (**Nancy**)
Card (**Ellen**)
Expensive, old-fashioned lawyer's type briefcase (**Brookner**)
Galley proof, pen (**Olivia**)
Tray with glass of whisky (**Ellen**)
Beach chair (**Danus**)
Picnic things (**Antonia** and **Penelope**)
Bright red sand bucket (**Penny**)
Stick, letter, envelope containing photograph (**Lawrence**)
Dog lead (**Nancy**)
Dog lead (**George**)
Holiday luggage (**Danus**)
Can of Coke (**Antonia**)
Rug, letter (**Penelope**)
Chairs (as required) (**All**)
Tray of drinks (**Noel**)
Case containing will and wrapped book with photograph, glasses, belongings (**Brookner**)

Personal: **Noel**: cigarettes, lighter
Penny: straw sun hat
Noel: silver ballpoint pen, small pocket notebook, calculator

LIGHTING PLOT

Property fittings required: nil
Various settings

ACT I   To open: Front lighting on gauze painting

Cue 1   When ready during music   (Page 1)
         Cross-fade to lighting on stage behind gauze

Cue 2   The sounds of the birds abate   (Page 1)
         Brings up lights on **Olivia** *and* **Nancy**

Cue 3   **Penelope** stands looking round after **Ellen** exits   (Page 2)
         Fade lights on **Penelope**

Cue 4   **Olivia**: "…should have been there when she got home."   (Page 2)
         Cross-fade to full lighting on conservatory

Cue 5   **Penelope** watches **Nancy** enter from conservatory   (Page 4)
         Bring up lighting on **Nancy** *and* **George**, *gradually fade*
           light on **Penelope**

Cue 6   **George** takes paper back and stares at it   (Page 6)
         Crossfade to **Penelope**

Cue 7   **Penelope**: "…through the open studio window——"   (Page 6)
         Bring up lights on **Lawrence** *and sea sky cyclorama*

Cue 8   Rumble of thunder is heard overhead   (Page 9)
         Fade lights, then bring up Blitz bombing lighting;
           spot light on **Penelope**

Cue 9   **Ellen** glances at **Penelope**   (Page 9)
         Fade lights on **Ellen** *and* **Penelope**, *bring up lights on*
           Olivia DS

Cue 10   **Olivia**: "…I think of last year in Ibiza."   (Page 12)
         Fade lights to shadow on **Olivia**'s *face; bring up clear,*
           hot Mediterranean light UR

Cue 11	**Penelope**: "Gracious heavens." *Pool of light on* **Antonia**, *while fading sunshine to black on* **Penelope** *and* **Olivia**	(Page 15)
Cue 12	Loud phone ringing *Cross-fade to* **Noel** DL	(Page 15)
Cue 13	**Ellen**: "Mrs Keeling?" *Lights up showing* **Ellen** *entering*	(Page 16)
Cue 14	**Olivia** leads **Noel** through conservatory *Cross-fade to opposite* DS *corner on* **Nancy** *and* **George**	(Page 25)
Cue 15	**Nancy**: "...at least have talked it over with me." *Bring up lights in conservatory*	(Page 26)
Cue 16	**Nancy**: "Think half a million *pounds*." *Lights down on* **Nancy** *and* **George**, *bring up lights *C *and* US	(Page 27)
Cue 17	**Antonia** looks at **Danus** *Lights down*	(Page 30)
Cue 18	After **Antonia** and **Danus** leave *Lights up*	(Page 30)
Cue 19	**Richard** and **Lawrence** look at each other *Fade lights down on them*	(Page 33)
Cue 20	**Penelope**: "...got him back playing backgammon..." *Lights up on the two men*	(Page 34)
Cue 21	**Richard** starts to set out the backgammon *Lights up on conservatory*	(Page 36)
Cue 22	**Richard** and **Lawrence** finish their game *Lights down, then front lighting on gauze painting*	(Page 37)
ACT II	To open: Cross-fade to lighting on stage behind gauze	
Cue 23	**Penelope**: "Nothing like a nice, new dress..." *Dim lights slightly on* **Penelope**, *bring up lights* DS	(Page 44)

Cue 24   Doorbell rings   (Page 45)
             Lights down on **Penny** *and* **Lawrence,** *up on* **Penelope**

Cue 25   **Penelope** answers phone, **Olivia** enters   (Page 48)
             Lights up on **Olivia**

Cue 26   **Olivia**: "Bye, darling. Bye."   (Page 49)
             Fade lights on **Olivia**

Cue 27   **Penelope** closes her eyes   (Page 52)
             Fade lights, leaving spot on **Penelope***; then* US *of*
             Penelope *bring up glow of a lit stove, suggesting*
             Lawrence*'s studio; evening, with a dark sky*

Cue 28   **Richard** and **Penny** kiss   (Page 53)
             Fade lights; then as sounds of battle come up and fade
             out, bring up lights on **Brookner**

Cue 29   **Brookner** raises his glass to **Penelope**   (Page 55)
             Fade to black; then lights up on **Nancy** *and* **Olivia**

Cue 30   **Olivia**: "Well, she has."   (Page 56)
             Bring lights up slowly US

Cue 31   **Olivia**: "I think you can imagine."   (Page 56)
             Fade lights on **Nancy** *and* **Olivia***, bring up sunshine* US

Cue 32   **Penelope**: "A very long time ago."   (Page 58)
             Fade lights, isolating **Penelope** *with* **Danus** *falling into*
             shadow

Cue 33   **Penelope**: "…it was a day just like today."   (Page 58)
             Bring up sunlight DS

Cue 34   Sounds of gulls and sea become muted   (Page 60)
             Fade lights to black, then bring up lights on **Penelope**
             and **Danus**

Cue 35   **Danus**: "Something not very good."   (Page 61)
             Cross-fade to **Nancy** *and* **George**

Cue 36   **George**: "If you know what's good for you."   (Page 62)
             Cross-fade to conservatory area

Cue 37   Sound of birdsong increases   (Page 65)
          Fade lights to black-out

Cue 38   **Olivia**: "I'm sorry, I really am."   (Page 65)
          Slowly bring up lights on **Penelope**

Cue 39   **Penny** enters   (Page 68)
          Change to warm summer sunlight on **Penny**

Cue 40   **Penelope** dies   (Page 69)
          Fade lights to black-out; when ready bring up lighting
          on stage

Cue 41   **Brookner** puts will in brief case   (Page 75)
          Lights down on conservatory

Cue 42   They raise their glasses and drink   (Page 78)
          Bring up lights on **Danus** *and* **Antonia** *in the*
          garden, and on **Penelope** *in her straw chair*

Cue 43   Sound of the sea and gulls   (Page 79)
          Slowly fade to black-out

EFFECTS PLOT

ACT I

Cue 1   To open Act I   (Page 1)
Music

Cue 2   **Penelope** enters   (Page 1)
Birdsong: crows and rooks in distant trees; fade

Cue 3   Lights go down on **Nancy** and **George**, up on **Penelope**   (Page 6)
Sounds of sea and gulls

Cue 4   Lights come up on **Lawrence**   (Page 6)
Chamberlain's announcement of war on radio as page 6

Cue 5   **Lawrence** turns radio off   (Page 7)
Cut radio sound

Cue 6   **Lawrence** and **Penny** stare into the distance   (Page 9)
*Rumble of thunder overhead, turning to sound of bombs
  falling and exploding until* **Penelope** *stands up, then
  change to birdsong and the quiet of countryside*

Cue 7   Lights fade on **Ellen** and **Penelope**   (Page 9)
Sound of voices and clatter of busy restaurant

Cue 8   Lighting changes to clear, hot Mediterranean light   (Page 12)
Sound of cicadas as well as distant faint wash of calm sea

Cue 9   **Antonia**: "Hi."   (Page 15)
Gust of wind

Cue 10   Sunshine fades to black on **Penelope** and **Olivia**   (Page 15)
*Sounds of party, glasses clinking, raised voices, fading
  under loud phone ringing*

Cue 11   **Ellen** begins to collect materials for a fire   (Page 17)
Noises from above

| *Cue* 12 | **Penelope**: "…friend of Olivia's I told you about——" | (Page 17) |
| | *Another mighty bump from upstairs* | |

| *Cue* 13 | **Ellen**: "What about him?" | (Page 17) |
| | *Knock on door, off* | |

| *Cue* 14 | **Ellen** exits | (Page 17) |
| | *More rumblings from above* | |

| *Cue* 15 | **Danus**: "I like gardening." | (Page 19) |
| | *Sound of car pulling up outside* | |

| *Cue* 16 | **Penelope**: "Good. Then how about…" | (Page 19) |
| | *Sound of door opening and closing* | |

| *Cue* 17 | **Penelope**: "She must be totally *bereft*." | (Page 21) |
| | *Another crash from upstairs* | |

| *Cue* 18 | Lights fade on **Nancy** and **George** | (Page 27) |
| | *Spring birdsong* | |

| *Cue* 19 | **Antonia**: "And not exactly amicably." | (Page 31) |
| | *Pinger sounds on timer on* **Penelope**'s *wrist* | |

| *Cue* 20 | **Penelope**: "…always mean something special to me…" | (Page 32) |
| | *Sound of seagulls cawing, ocean breaking on shore* | |

ACT II

| *Cue* 21 | **Penny** shows her dress. **Lawrence** smiles | (Page 45) |
| | *Doorbell rings* | |

| *Cue* 22 | **Penelope**: "…could no longer hold his brushes." | (Page 48) |
| | *Phone rings* | |

Cue 23	Lights fade leaving **Penelope** lit in single spot	(Page 52)
	Sounds of crashing sea waves and call of circling gulls,	
	then just the sound of the wind and the seas	

Cue 24	**Penny** and **Richard** kiss	(Page 53)
	Sound of sea below studio, magnified, then sound of	
	war, of guns, machine guns, rifles, big guns, sound of	
	battle until it reaches almost deafening proportion, then fade	

Cue 27	**Penelope:** "...it was a day just like today." *Increase sound of sea, waves breaking on shore, sound of sea breeze and cry of gulls*	(Page 58)
Cue 28	**Penelope** performs silent scream *Cry of seagull overhead, becoming hugely amplified, joined by screeching of many seagulls; sounds of gulls and sea become muted as lights fade to black; chatter of gulls rises then fades as lights come back up*	(Page 60)
Cue 29	**Danus** enters *Sound of taxi driving off*	(Page 62)
Cue 30	**Antonia** and **Penelope** embrace *Sound of birdsong increases; music—single solo cello*	(Page 65)
Cue 31	**Penelope:** "...curling over the beach like smoke——" *Faint fret from sea blowing in from other side*	(Page 68)
Cue 32	**Richard** enters *Fret begins to clear*	(Page 69)
Cue 33	**Penelope** dies *Voice of Vera Lynn singing "We'll Meet Again"*	(Page 69)
Cue 34	**Young Couple** embrace *Sound of sea, crashing of its waves and calling of seagulls*	(Page 79)

MADE AND PRINTED IN GREAT BRITAIN BY
LATIMER TREND & COMPANY LTD PLYMOUTH
MADE IN ENGLAND